DONALD TRUMP ANNUAL 2019

ADAM G GOODWIN
JONATHAN PARKYN

100%
UNOFFICIAL

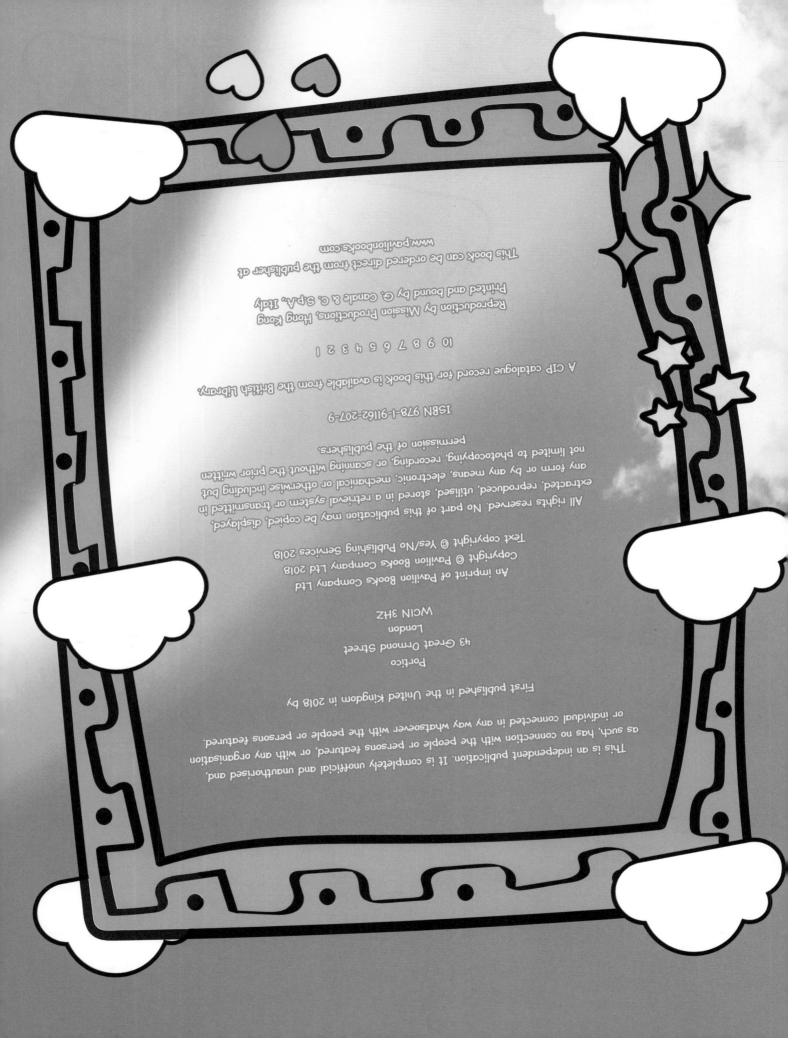

First published in the United Kingdom in 2018 by

Portico
43 Great Ormond Street
London
WC1N 3HZ

An imprint of Pavilion Books Company Ltd

ISBN 978-1-91162-207-9

A CIP catalogue record for this book is available from the British Library.

10 9 8 7 6 5 4 3 2 1

Reproduction by Mission Productions, Hong Kong
Printed and bound by G. Canale & C. S.p.A., Italy

This book can be ordered direct from the publisher at
www.pavilionbooks.com

THIS BOOK BELONGS TO
NAME
....
AGE
....

CONTENTS

Hey, Kids! ... 6
Trump's Gang – Donald Trump ... 7
'Wrestling with his Destiny' Photostory ... 8
Trump's Gang – Vladimir Putin ... 13
Trumpunzel's Trumpuzzle ... 14
Dear Donald! ... 16
Splice Your Own Trumpanzee ... 18
Donald's 'Quest for Adventure' Adventure ... 20
Trump's Gang – Kim Jong-un ... 23
Steaks and Ladders Game ... 24
Pin the Quiff on the Donald Game ... 26
Cut-out-and-Keep Dancing Donald ... 28
Donald Word Search ... 30
Donald's 'Hair Flair' Salon ... 32
Trump's Gang – Stormy Daniels ... 34
Cut-out-and-Keep Fun Mask – Donald Trump ... 35
Cut-out-and-Keep Fun Mask – Kim Jong-un ... 37
I Believe in Miracles ... 39
Pull My Finger ... 40
Don't Stop Believing ... 42

CONTENTS

Trump's Gang – Steve Bannon 43
Face Time with Donald 44
Delicious Donald's Party Treats 46
Other Dishy Donalds 48
Donny's 'Put a Pin in it' Fake News Balloon Game 50
Trump's True Colours 52
Trump's Gang – Hillary Clinton 54
The Three Little Trumps, and the Big Bad Wolff 55
Donald's Pony Care Tips 58
Don's Gone Golfin' Game 60
'The Apprentice of Love' Photostory 62
Make 'Everything' Great Again Kit 67
Sheriff Trump 70
Don't Make Donald Cross(word) 72
Trump's Gang – Barack Obama 74
The Speeding Phantom A Locker Room Gang Mystery 75
Answers 78
Photo Credits 80

WELCOME!

Hey Kids!

It's the editor here! What a so, so, special world it is at the moment. Can you believe that Donald has proven everyone wrong and is living in a real-life fairytale? Dreams really can come true, and with a whole bunch of wishing and a teensy bit of luck you can make your dreams come true too – just like Donald did!

Within this enchanted annual you will find fun facts and data in Trump's Gang, the romantic photostories The Apprentice of Love and Wrestling With his Destiny, puzzling puzzles, wonderful word searches and the Don't Get Donald Cross(word). Not only this, but also short stories to beguile and amaze, fantastic fun masks to cut out and keep, the Pin the Quiff on the Donald game, top advice in Face Time with Donald and colour me good with Trump's True Colours! And so, so, so much more!

And remember, if you keep on believing then your dreams might come true too!

Big hugs,

The Editor

ALWAYS 100% UNOFFICIAL

TRUMP'S GANG

Donald Trump

HAIR:	LUSTROUS
CUTENESS:	🐱🐱🐱🐱🐱
FAVOURITE COLOUR:	RAINBOW
SPARKLE RATING:	☆☆☆☆☆
KINDFULNESS:	110%
POLITICAL STRENGTH:	10/10
FRIENDSHIP FACTOR:	♥♥♥♥♥

SPECIAL POWER:
DONALD SENDS OUT PULSES OF PURE LOVE WHEN HE SMILES!!

TRUMP LOVE STORY
WRESTLING WITH HIS DESTINY
STARRING the young JULIAN SANDS as the young DONALD TRUMP
Tough hunk Donnie Trump arrived in Palm Beach with only his leather blouson and a suitcase full of regrets...
THE HEAT GOT TOO HOT IN QUEENS WITH THAT FLICK KNIFE GANG AFTER ME. SWELL PETE WON'T FIND ME HERE!
Bad boy Donnie wanted to put Queens behind him and start afresh in Palm Beach, Florida...
SURE, I'VE GOT A ROOM TO RENT, HONEY. FIFTY BUCKS A NIGHT, FULL ENGLISH INCLUDED. YOU GOOD FOR THE DOUGH?
I SURE AM, MRS LOPEZ. I MIGHT BE A BAD APPLE FROM THE BIG APPLE, BUT I'VE ALWAYS HAD A WAY WITH MONEY!
CAREFUL ON THOSE STAIRS, HONEY. THEY'RE QUITE STEEP!
DON'T WORRY, MRS LOPEZ. STAIRS DON'T BOTHER ME.

I'VE DONE SOME FLIPPING BAD STUFF, BUT STEALING FROM SWELL PETE...
...THAT WAS THE FLIPPING WORST! HIS FLICK KNIFE GANG WILL NEVER GIVE UP TILL THEY STAB ME IN THE TUMMY!
AND ALL BECAUSE I STOLE SWELL PETE'S FAVOURITE SHELL...
IT'S SO BEAUTIFUL! AND IF I PUT IT TO MY EAR, I CAN HEAR THE BUSY HUBBUB AND THRUM OF QUEENS!
Later, daydreaming on the beach...
I DIDN'T REALISE PALM BEACH WAS GOING TO BE SO PEBBLY. IF I'D KNOWN I'D HAVE BROUGHT MY FAVOURITE FLIPPING FLIP-FLOPS!
HEY! WHERE DID THAT GIRL COME FROM? SHE'S GOT FLIP-FLOPS. I WONDER WHERE SHE BOUGHT THEM?
The pebbles were hurting his knees.
WAIT! WHERE DID YOU GET YOUR FLIP-FLOPS FROM?
WHAT? OH! PRIMARK!
I REALLY LIKE YOUR HANDS!
OH, THANKS! I CREAM THEM EVERY DAY. THERE'S A PRIMARK ON RODEO BOULEVARD IF YOU WANT FLIP-FLOPS LIKE MINE.
I REALLY LOVE FLIP-FLOPS. AND SHELLS, TOO.
REALLY? SAME! WE'VE GOT SO MUCH IN COMMON!
Though they'd had fun, the pair agreed to go their separate ways...
...but then changed their minds and went for a beach coffee together.
THANKS FOR THE BEACH COFFEE. MY NAME'S DONNIE, BY THE WAY. WHAT'S YOURS?
MY NAME'S DESTINY. I RECOGNISE YOUR ACCENT. YOU'RE FROM QUEENS, TOO. MAYBE IN A DIFFERENT LIFE WE COULD HAVE BEEN FRIENDS. OR MAYBE SOMETHING MORE. LIKE... LOVERS!

GOSH! THAT'S A BIT FORWARD! WE'VE ONLY JUST SHARED A BEACH COFFEE TOGETHER. AND NOW YOU'RE TOUCHING MY ARM!
I EMBARRASSED YOU, DIDN'T I? SORRY, DONNIE, IT'S JUST THAT I'M TRAPPED IN A LOVELESS RELATIONSHIP WITH A TERRIBLE MAN AND CRAVE SENSUAL RELEASE!
PEPSI
ANYWAY, I'VE GOT TO GO NOW. IT'S TIME FOR ME TO CREAM MY HANDS AGAIN. SEE YA!
OK, THEN! THANK YOU FOR TOUCHING MY ARM!
Several cups of beach coffee and a Cornetto later, Donnie saw Destiny again – this time she was with another man!
THAT MUST BE THE TERRIBLE MAN DESTINY SAID SHE WAS TRAPPED WITH. BUT I CAN'T SEE HIS FACE... SHE TOUCHED MY ARM – AND MY HEART. BUT NOW SHE'S TOUCHING HIS RIBS.
MAYBE I'LL HEAD DOWN TO RODEO BOULEVARD AND GET ME SOME SWEET FLIP-FLOPS!
Donnie realised he needed to try and forget about Destiny. He also realised he needed to buy some swimming trunks from Primark...
...But the next day, with his new trunks in a towel, Donnie couldn't get Destiny out of his mind.
SHE'S HAUNTING MY BRAIN LIKE A BEAUTIFUL GHOST. I CAN'T THINK OF ANYONE ELSE!
GUESS WHO!
I'D KNOW THOSE HANDS ANYWHERE! MRS LOPEZ, IT'S YOU!!
But it wasn't Mrs Lopez at all. It was Destiny – in her bikini again!
IS MRS LOPEZ YOUR GIRLFRIEND? YOU CAN BE HONEST WITH ME!
UGH! NO WAY! THE THOUGHT OF IT HAS MADE ME FEEL REALLY SICK.
Donnie immediately puked into his towel.
JESUS, DONNIE, THAT STINKS! I THINK I'M GONNA BARF TOO!
SORRY ABOUT THAT!

I KNOW – LET'S DO SOME WRESTLING. LIKE THIS... SMACKDOWN!
I LOVE WRESTLING, TOO. AND ROUGHHOUSING! YOU'RE PINNING ME TO THE CANVAS!
I WANT TO KNOW EVERYTHING ABOUT YOU
LET ME WHISPER A SECRET... I THINK I'VE GOT A PEBBLE UP MY BUM...
COME ON, DONNIE. STOP CHANGING THE SUBJECT.
OK, LOOK. I'VE DONE SOMETHING REALLY TERRIBLE IN MY PAST.
BUT YOU'RE SO HUNKY! WHAT COULD YOU HAVE DONE THAT'S SO BAD?
I STOLE A SEA OBJECT FROM SOMEONE VIOLENT. I CAN NEVER GO BACK TO QUEENS.
SOUNDS TERRIBLE. ANYWAY, GOTTA CREAM MY HANDS AGAIN. THESE BABIES DON'T SOFTEN THEMSELVES!
SWEET DREAMS, TOOTS!
The next day they wore clothes...
THESE RIGID, UNYIELDING POLES REMIND ME OF MY LOVELESS RELATIONSHIP
THINK, DONNIE! THERE MUST BE A WAY YOU CAN CHEER HER UP... I KNOW!
Suddenly, out of nowhere, Donnie grabbed Destiny by the chest.
SMACKDOWN! YOU'RE GOING DOWNTOWN!!
WHEEEEEEE!
But soon the wrestling started to get a bit out of hand....
THIS IS MY SIGNATURE MOVE – IT'S CALLED THE LOVE BITE!
OH DONNIE, YOU'RE WINNING THE CHAMPIONSHIP BELT OF MY HEART!
But it couldn't last...
...it was time to face facts.
OH, DESTINY, I'VE FALLEN INTO YOUR HEART AND I'M DROWNING IN LOVE!
BUT IT CAN'T GO ON! ALTHOUGH MY HEART BELONGS TO YOU, MY BODY AND HANDS BELONG TO ANOTHER, REMEMBER?
Their hearts were breaking like the waves on the beach...

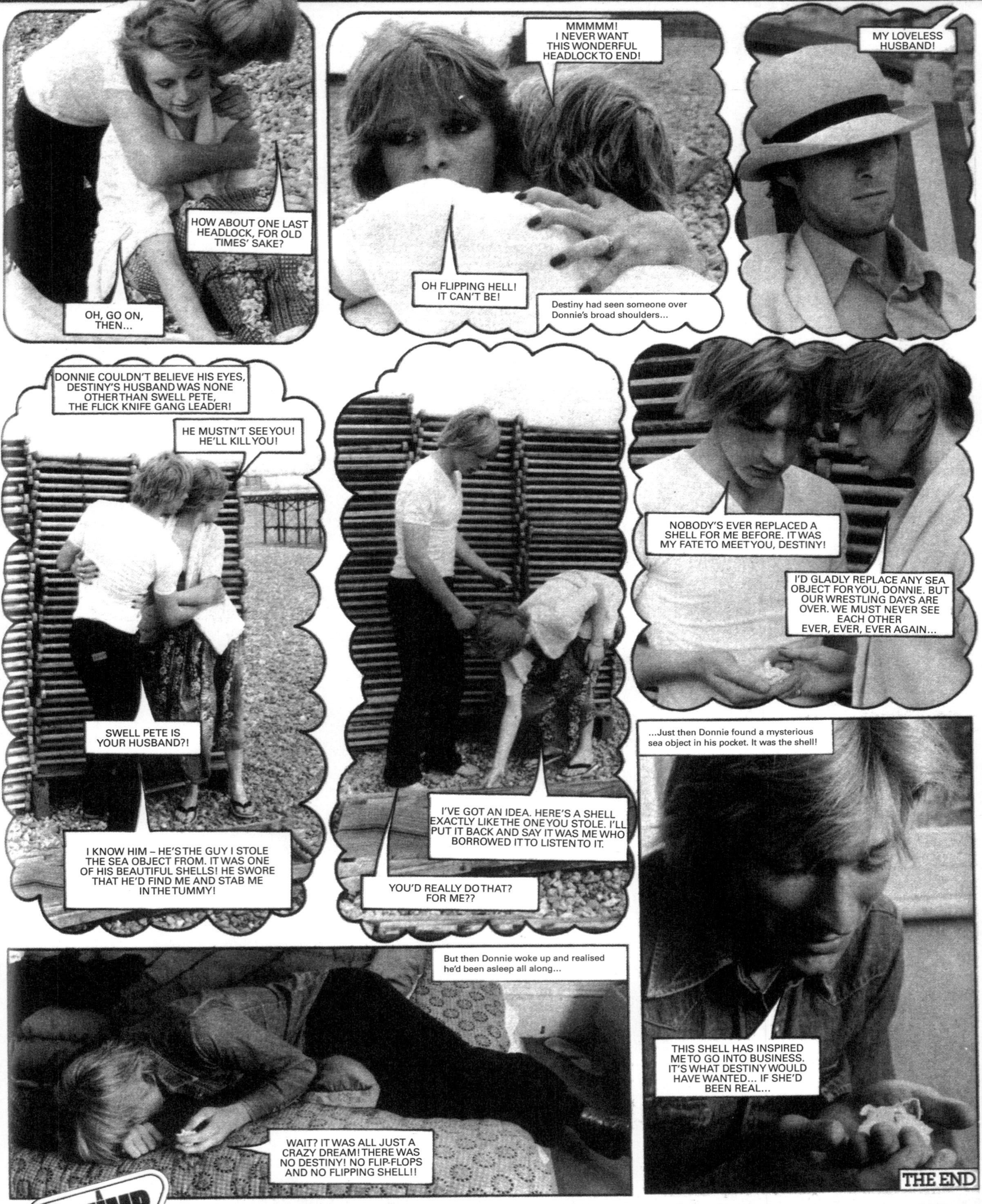
HOW ABOUT ONE LAST HEADLOCK, FOR OLD TIMES' SAKE?
OH, GO ON, THEN...
MMMMM! I NEVER WANT THIS WONDERFUL HEADLOCK TO END!
OH FLIPPING HELL! IT CAN'T BE!
Destiny had seen someone over Donnie's broad shoulders...
MY LOVELESS HUSBAND!
DONNIE COULDN'T BELIEVE HIS EYES, DESTINY'S HUSBAND WAS NONE OTHER THAN SWELL PETE, THE FLICK KNIFE GANG LEADER!
HE MUSTN'T SEE YOU! HE'LL KILL YOU!
SWELL PETE IS YOUR HUSBAND?!
I KNOW HIM – HE'S THE GUY I STOLE THE SEA OBJECT FROM. IT WAS ONE OF HIS BEAUTIFUL SHELLS! HE SWORE THAT HE'D FIND ME AND STAB ME IN THE TUMMY!
I'VE GOT AN IDEA. HERE'S A SHELL EXACTLY LIKE THE ONE YOU STOLE. I'LL PUT IT BACK AND SAY IT WAS ME WHO BORROWED IT TO LISTEN TO IT.
YOU'D REALLY DO THAT? FOR ME??
NOBODY'S EVER REPLACED A SHELL FOR ME BEFORE. IT WAS MY FATE TO MEET YOU, DESTINY!
I'D GLADLY REPLACE ANY SEA OBJECT FOR YOU, DONNIE. BUT OUR WRESTLING DAYS ARE OVER. WE MUST NEVER SEE EACH OTHER EVER, EVER, EVER AGAIN...
But then Donnie woke up and realised he'd been asleep all along...
WAIT? IT WAS ALL JUST A CRAZY DREAM! THERE WAS NO DESTINY! NO FLIP-FLOPS AND NO FLIPPING SHELL!!
...Just then Donnie found a mysterious sea object in his pocket. It was the shell!
THIS SHELL HAS INSPIRED ME TO GO INTO BUSINESS. IT'S WHAT DESTINY WOULD HAVE WANTED... IF SHE'D BEEN REAL...
THE END

TRUMP'S GANG

Vladimir Putin

HAIR:	SOME
CUTENESS:	😻
FAVOURITE COLOUR:	RED
SPARKLE RATING:	☆ ☆
KINDFULNESS:	42%
POLITICAL STRENGTH:	9/10
FRIENDSHIP FACTOR:	♥ ♥ ♥ ♥

SPECIAL POWER:
VLADIMIR HAS THE STRENGTH
OF TWENTY STALLIONS!!

Whilst letting down his long, blond hair

Donald Trumpunzel

has pricked his finger on the spindle of a nearby spinning wheel, sending him into a deep and business-like slumber.

YOU are an enchanted frog and **YOU** must choose the correct strand of golden hair to hop up Trump Tower and awaken your sleeping prince with a

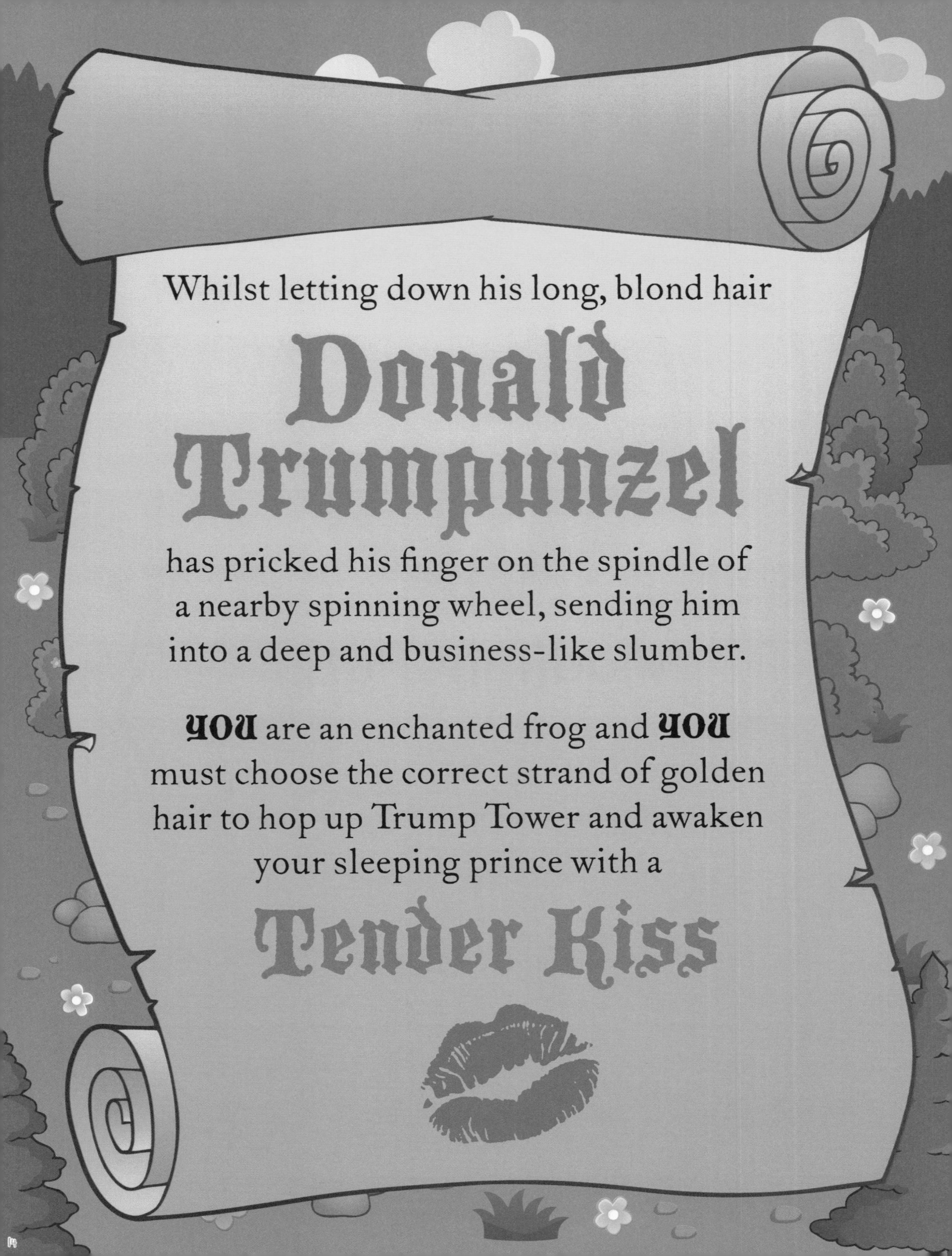

Tender Kiss

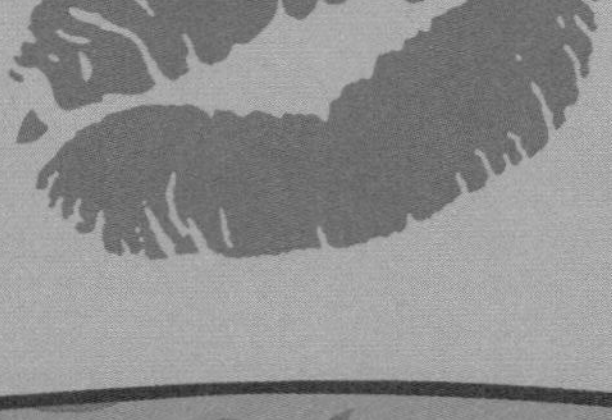

Dear DONALD!

As a stable genius, Donald Trump seems to have an answer for everything. But what about questions of the heart? Here's some of the brilliant advice that Donald might have given people, had he been a famous Agony Uncle instead of a famous Business Tycoon or a famous President of the United States.

SHOULD I TELL HER HOW I FEEL?

Dear Donald,

I think I'm in love with my best friend's friend. She's beautiful and clever and I want to ask her out, but I'm worried she only thinks of me as her friend's best friend and not a boyfriend. To make matters worse, her other friend's boyfriend's brother is also my brother's best friend's sister's boyfriend! So, you can see my problem. Please help!

Bobby D (16)

Hitchin

WHAT MIGHT DONALD SAY?

Phew! Your love life sounds very, very, very complicated, Bobby. So, so complicated. It's about as difficult to unravel as one of my business's tax returns! If I were you, I'd just come right out and tell your gal how you feel about her. You never know – maybe she feels the same way about you, too! But if she doesn't think you're boyfriend material, then sue her for defamation of character. That'll make her notice you!

IS THE PARTY OVER?

Dear Donald,

How do you tell someone you don't love them any more? My bf used to be all like 'hey, Gina, let's go dancing' or 'come on, hun, there's this totally banging party and everyone's gonna be there'. He used to be, like, Mister Fun Guy, 24/7. But since we've moved in together, all he ever does is watch *Game of Thrones* and play video games and eat a lot. I mean, a LOT. He's, like, suddenly the boringest, you know? Plus he picks his nose. Plus I've met someone else.

Gina (22)

(via Snapchat)

WHAT MIGHT DONALD SAY?

Well, if this was an episode of my highly successful TV show The Apprentice, *I'd tell you to say 'you're fired!' to that lazy so and so, and give this new fella of yours a high-up job in your company instead. So, so high-up in your company. But this isn't an episode of my highly successful TV show* The Apprentice, *so my advice would be to try and talk to your boyfriend. Open your heart to him. See if you and he can find some common ground and maybe rekindle some of that magical spark you both once felt. And if that doesn't work, then you can tell him he's fired.*

CAN YOU LEND A 'HELPING' HAND?

Dear Donald,

I'm thinking of going into big business – maybe real estate, or maybe opening a chain of hotels, or building some casinos, or all three. I haven't decided yet. The point is that, although I'm very good at business, I suffer from confidence issues relating to my overly hairy hands. As you probably know, in the high-flying business world, a lot of deals are sealed with a handshake. I'm worried that one look at my furry paws will send prospective clients and financiers running to the hills! I've tried shaving my hands, but that just makes them stubbly. And waxing is so painful it makes me feel sick. Any suggestions?

Andy O'Hare (47)

Chicago

WHAT MIGHT DONALD SAY?

Confidence is so, so important in business – as it is in life. And it's so, so easy for embarrassing personal conditions such as yours to undermine your success by making you feel doubtful and uncertain. What I would say to you is this: embrace your disadvantages and allow them to make you strong. Be proud of yourself, no matter what. Don't listen to the haters – rise above them. And, eventually, you'll discover that you've become so powerful and successful that everyone will have to do what you say, no matter how weird your hands are.

TRUMPENSTEIN'S LABORATORY

Donald is so rich that he could set up his own research facility and pay a bunch of scientific eggheads to splice his genes with those of his favourite primate – the cheeky chimpanzee. Now, imagine Donald's research facility is real, and you're the brainbox boffin that he has put in charge. Carefully cut out Donald's face and hair, and then 'splice' the images together using sticky tape or paper glue.

Congratulations! You've created the world's first
TRUMPANZEE!

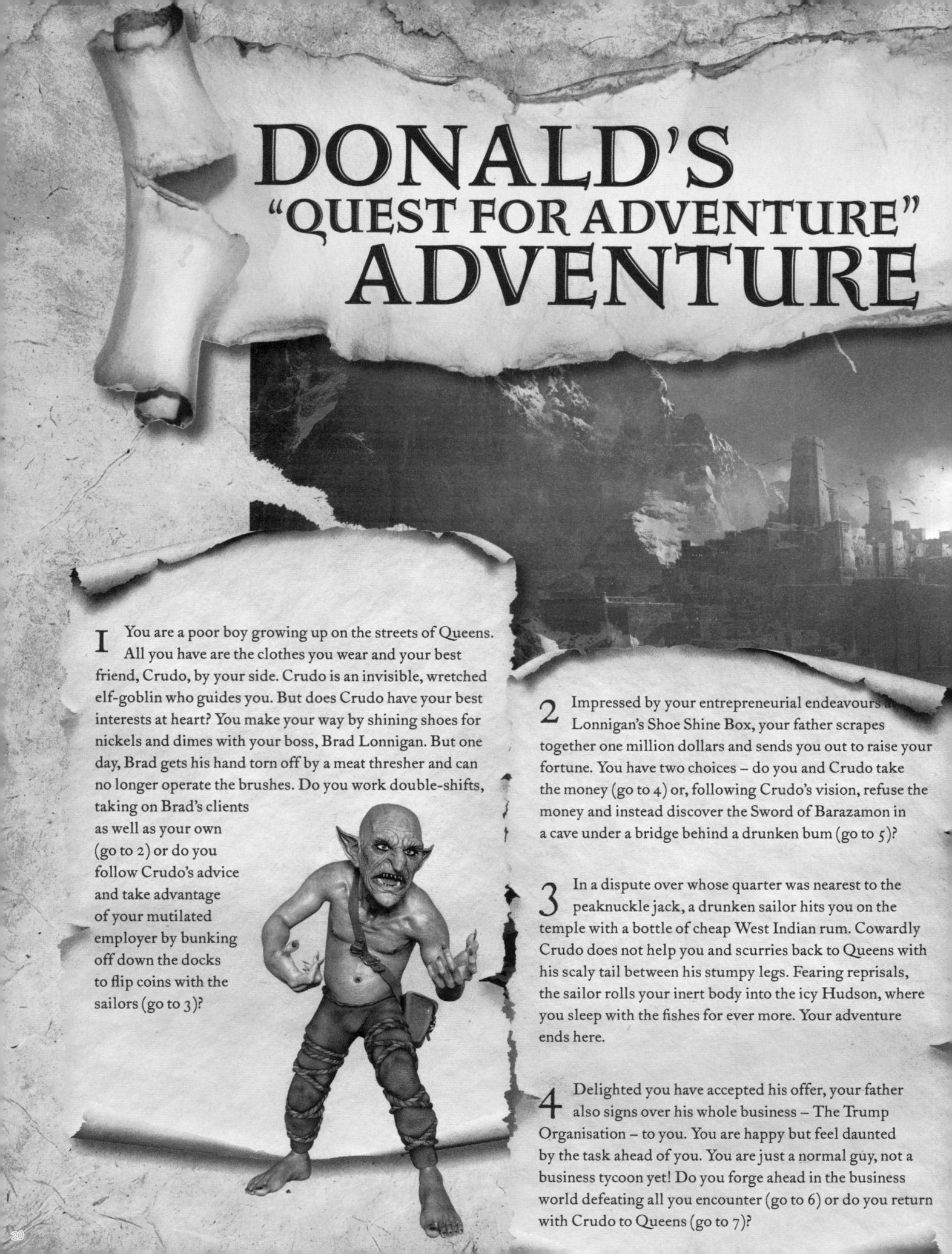

DONALD'S "QUEST FOR ADVENTURE" ADVENTURE

1 You are a poor boy growing up on the streets of Queens. All you have are the clothes you wear and your best friend, Crudo, by your side. Crudo is an invisible, wretched elf-goblin who guides you. But does Crudo have your best interests at heart? You make your way by shining shoes for nickels and dimes with your boss, Brad Lonnigan. But one day, Brad gets his hand torn off by a meat thresher and can no longer operate the brushes. Do you work double-shifts, taking on Brad's clients as well as your own (go to 2) or do you follow Crudo's advice and take advantage of your mutilated employer by bunking off down the docks to flip coins with the sailors (go to 3)?

2 Impressed by your entrepreneurial endeavours at Lonnigan's Shoe Shine Box, your father scrapes together one million dollars and sends you out to raise your fortune. You have two choices – do you and Crudo take the money (go to 4) or, following Crudo's vision, refuse the money and instead discover the Sword of Barazamon in a cave under a bridge behind a drunken bum (go to 5)?

3 In a dispute over whose quarter was nearest to the peaknuckle jack, a drunken sailor hits you on the temple with a bottle of cheap West Indian rum. Cowardly Crudo does not help you and scurries back to Queens with his scaly tail between his stumpy legs. Fearing reprisals, the sailor rolls your inert body into the icy Hudson, where you sleep with the fishes for ever more. Your adventure ends here.

4 Delighted you have accepted his offer, your father also signs over his whole business – The Trump Organisation – to you. You are happy but feel daunted by the task ahead of you. You are just a normal guy, not a business tycoon yet! Do you forge ahead in the business world defeating all you encounter (go to 6) or do you return with Crudo to Queens (go to 7)?

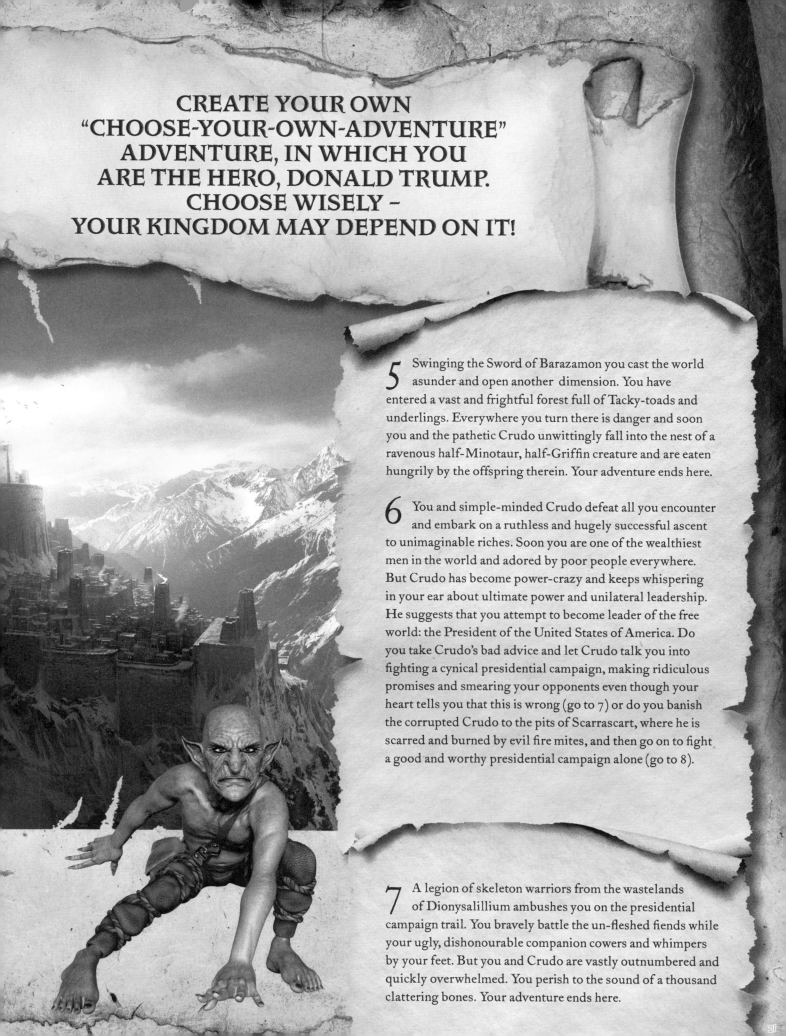

CREATE YOUR OWN "CHOOSE-YOUR-OWN-ADVENTURE" ADVENTURE, IN WHICH YOU ARE THE HERO, DONALD TRUMP. CHOOSE WISELY – YOUR KINGDOM MAY DEPEND ON IT!

5 Swinging the Sword of Barazamon you cast the world asunder and open another dimension. You have entered a vast and frightful forest full of Tacky-toads and underlings. Everywhere you turn there is danger and soon you and the pathetic Crudo unwittingly fall into the nest of a ravenous half-Minotaur, half-Griffin creature and are eaten hungrily by the offspring therein. Your adventure ends here.

6 You and simple-minded Crudo defeat all you encounter and embark on a ruthless and hugely successful ascent to unimaginable riches. Soon you are one of the wealthiest men in the world and adored by poor people everywhere. But Crudo has become power-crazy and keeps whispering in your ear about ultimate power and unilateral leadership. He suggests that you attempt to become leader of the free world: the President of the United States of America. Do you take Crudo's bad advice and let Crudo talk you into fighting a cynical presidential campaign, making ridiculous promises and smearing your opponents even though your heart tells you that this is wrong (go to 7) or do you banish the corrupted Crudo to the pits of Scarrascart, where he is scarred and burned by evil fire mites, and then go on to fight a good and worthy presidential campaign alone (go to 8).

7 A legion of skeleton warriors from the wastelands of Dionysalillium ambushes you on the presidential campaign trail. You bravely battle the un-fleshed fiends while your ugly, dishonourable companion cowers and whimpers by your feet. But you and Crudo are vastly outnumbered and quickly overwhelmed. You perish to the sound of a thousand clattering bones. Your adventure ends here.

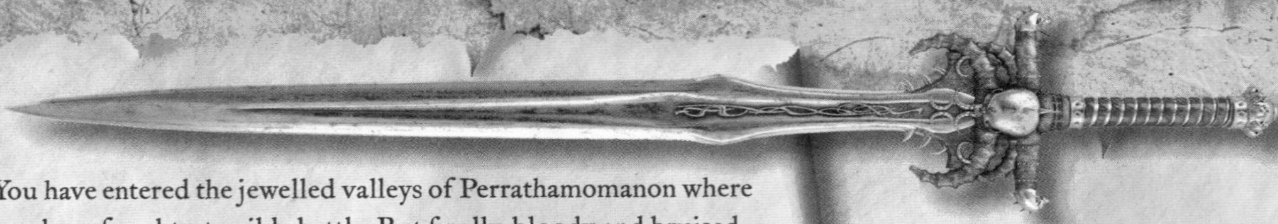

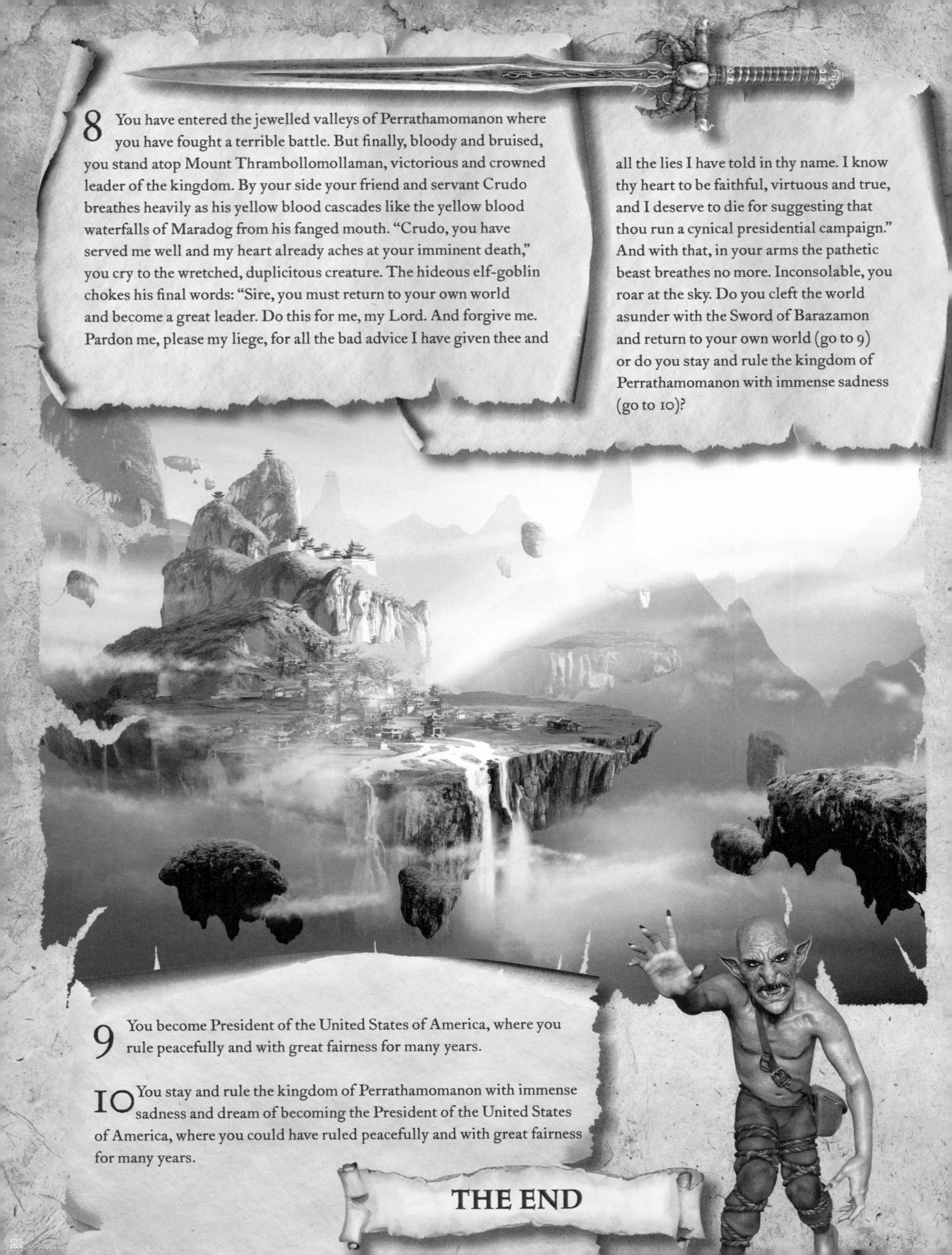

8 You have entered the jewelled valleys of Perrathamomanon where you have fought a terrible battle. But finally, bloody and bruised, you stand atop Mount Thrambollomollaman, victorious and crowned leader of the kingdom. By your side your friend and servant Crudo breathes heavily as his yellow blood cascades like the yellow blood waterfalls of Maradog from his fanged mouth. "Crudo, you have served me well and my heart already aches at your imminent death," you cry to the wretched, duplicitous creature. The hideous elf-goblin chokes his final words: "Sire, you must return to your own world and become a great leader. Do this for me, my Lord. And forgive me. Pardon me, please my liege, for all the bad advice I have given thee and all the lies I have told in thy name. I know thy heart to be faithful, virtuous and true, and I deserve to die for suggesting that thou run a cynical presidential campaign." And with that, in your arms the pathetic beast breathes no more. Inconsolable, you roar at the sky. Do you cleft the world asunder with the Sword of Barazamon and return to your own world (go to 9) or do you stay and rule the kingdom of Perrathamomanon with immense sadness (go to 10)?

9 You become President of the United States of America, where you rule peacefully and with great fairness for many years.

10 You stay and rule the kingdom of Perrathamomanon with immense sadness and dream of becoming the President of the United States of America, where you could have ruled peacefully and with great fairness for many years.

THE END

TRUMP'S GANG

Kim Jong-un

HAIR:	SHINY
CUTENESS:	🐱🐱🐱🐱
FAVOURITE COLOUR:	FUCHSIA
SPARKLE RATING:	☆☆☆☆☆
KINDFULNESS:	12%
POLITICAL STRENGTH:	9/10
FRIENDSHIP FACTOR:	♥

SPECIAL POWER:
KIM CAN BURROW UNDERGROUND
AT GREAT SPEED!!

Steaks And Ladders!

You've heard of 'Snakes and Ladders', now try Donald Trump's very own version — 'Steaks and Ladders', named after his short-lived mail-order steak business, Trump Steaks

Cut out the elevator 'counters', roll the dice and be the first to scale the wibbly-wobbly Trump Tower. Try to climb those ladders and head up to the penthouse suite on the 48th floor — but avoid landing on those juicy, rare, bloody steaks or you'll slip back down to the lobby!

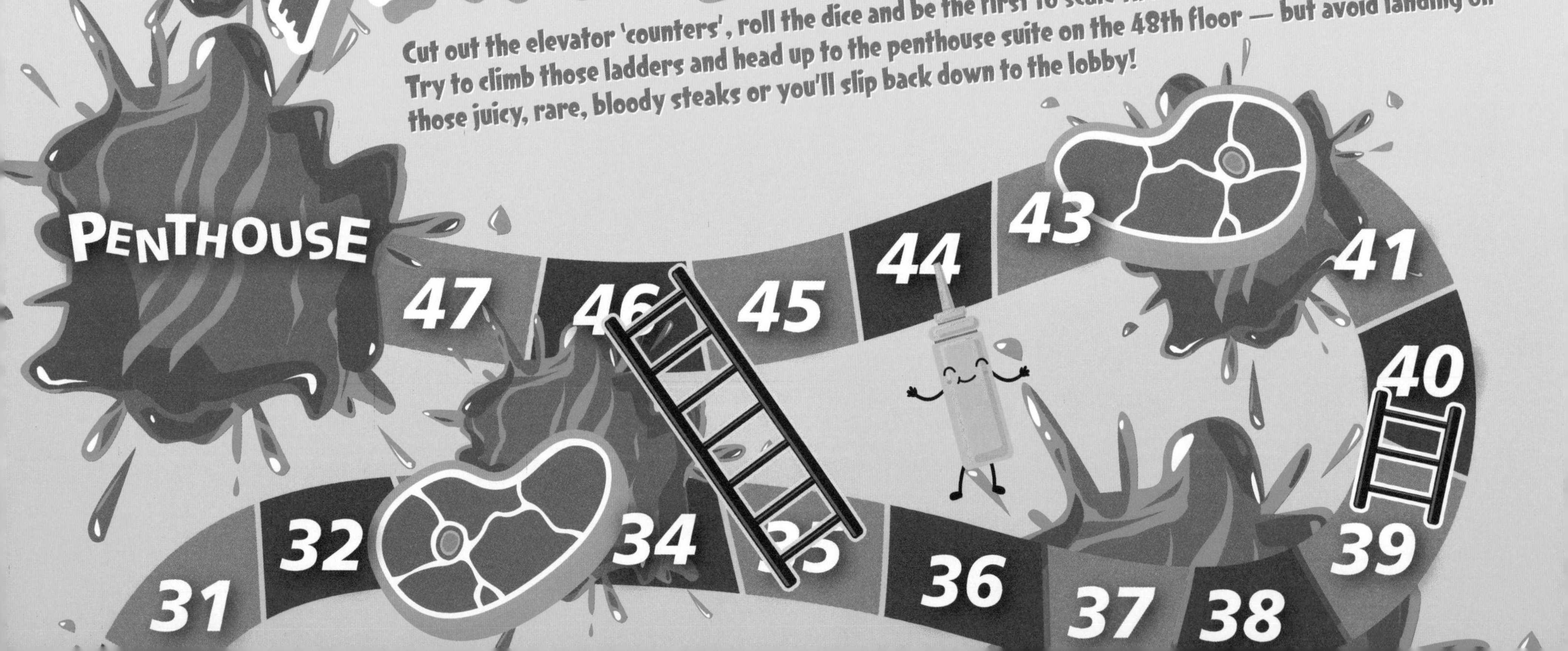

LOBBY
1
2
3
4
5
6
8
9
10
11
12
13
14
15
17
18
19
20
21
22
23
24
26
27
28
30

PIN THE QUIFF
ON THE
DONALD

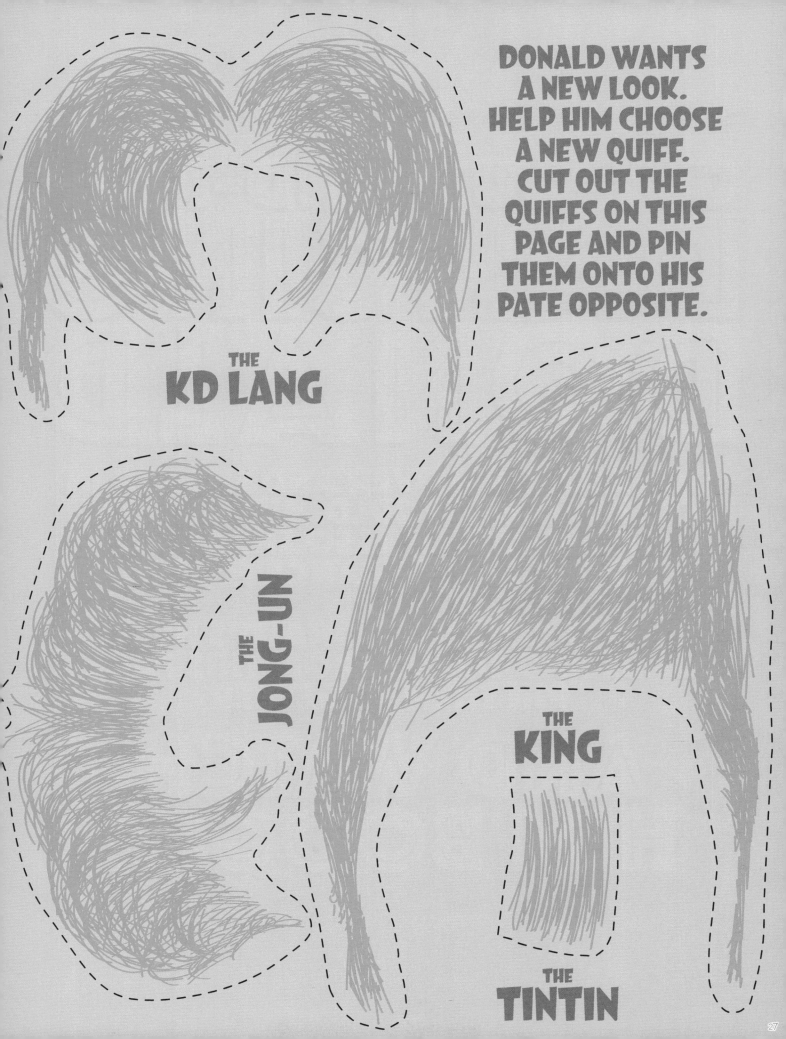

DONALD WANTS A NEW LOOK. HELP HIM CHOOSE A NEW QUIFF. CUT OUT THE QUIFFS ON THIS PAGE AND PIN THEM ONTO HIS PATE OPPOSITE.

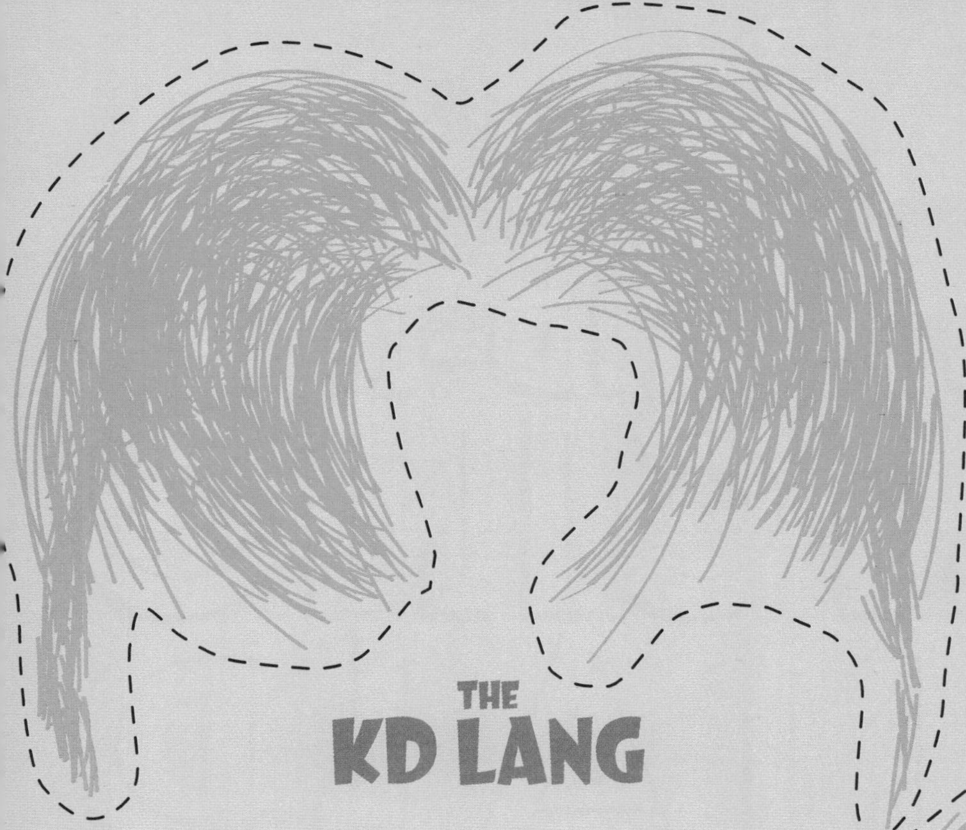

THE **KD LANG**

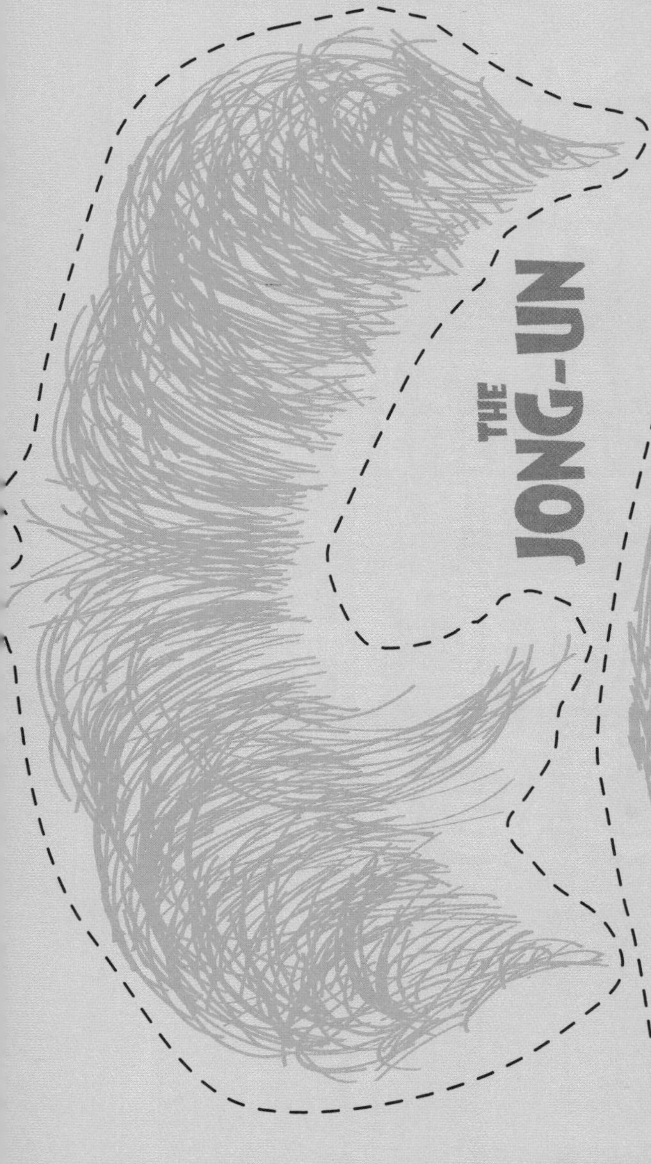

THE **JONG-UN**

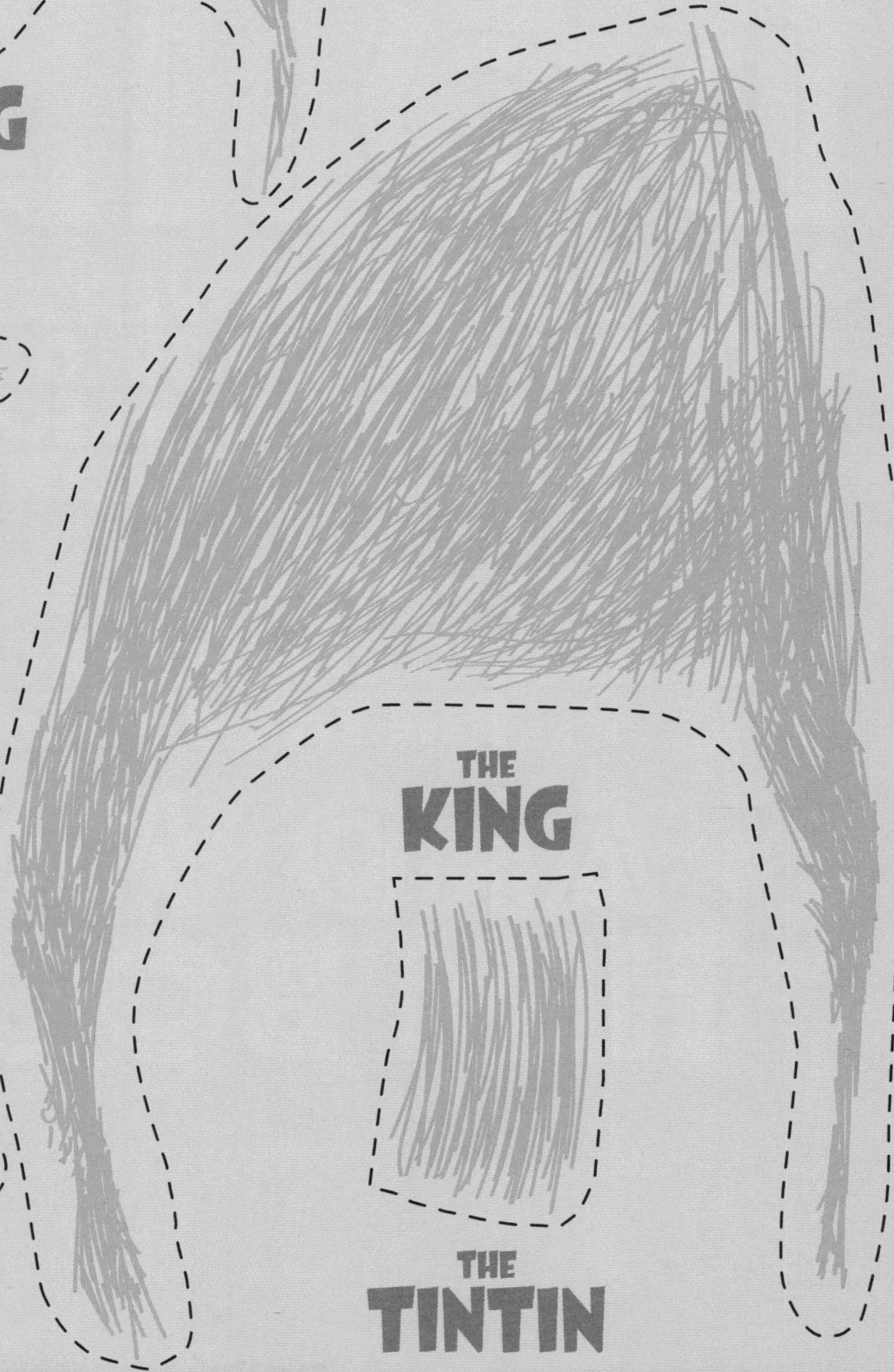

THE **KING**

THE **TINTIN**

CUT-OUT-AND-KEEP

DANCING DONALD

DONALD IS A MOVER AND SHAKER IN THE BUSINESS WORLD. BUT DID YOU KNOW HE CAN ALSO SHAKE HIS BOOTY ON THE DANCE FLOOR?

SIMPLY CUT OUT DONALD'S HEAD, LIMBS AND TORSO FROM THIS PAGE, PIN THEM TOGETHER

AND WATCH HIM BOOGIE!

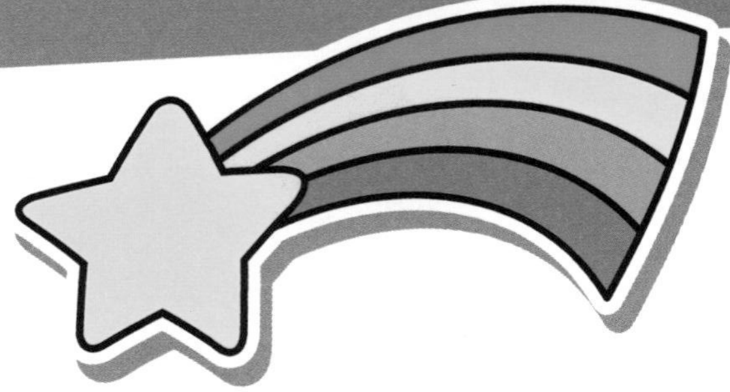

Q	S	Y	A	I	S	S	U	R	B	H	A	I	R
U	E	S	T	A	T	E	A	R	N	O	C	L	N
E	C	Z	M	I	S	B	G	Z	I	T	V	K	S
E	I	Z	C	B	S	L	O	C	K	E	R	C	N
N	T	T	M	S	P	R	V	J	F	L	O	G	O
S	N	L	S	I	A	M	E	L	A	N	I	A	I
N	E	Q	A	F	L	J	U	V	B	V	Y	Y	L
A	R	O	O	M	G	L	Z	R	I	G	H	T	L
M	P	E	N	C	E	S	I	T	V	N	E	C	I
R	P	E	N	O	L	A	E	O	A	K	U	S	B
E	A	E	R	O	K	J	K	O	N	I	S	A	C
G	E	M	N	S	E	M	O	H	A	L	R	A	M

DONALD WORD SEARCH

Donald's making a speech and keeps forgetting his words. Stop him looking stupid by finding them for him.

HOTEL UNIVERSITY FAR RIGHT ESTATE GOLF IVANA MELANIA MARLA APPRENTICE KOREA RUSSIA PENCE SO MILLION BILLIONS HAIR CASINO NRA ALONE ALT LOCKER ROOM GERMAN QUEENS.

DONALD'S 'HAIR FLAIR' SALON

Donald is world renowned for his beautiful, lustrous head of hair. How does he keep it looking so great? The truth is, that no one really knows. But here are some possible tips that Donald might share – if he wasn't too busy running the Western World!

1

The special night out

If you're heading out and you want a bit of extra sparkle, why not add some glitter to your favourite hair gel. You'll dazzle in those bright lights.

2

The photo op

The last thing you want when the world's press is on your doorstep is to look a mess. Make sure when you face the lenses that you're standing down wind of your fringe. You don't want to risk the 'trap door' rising unexpectedly.

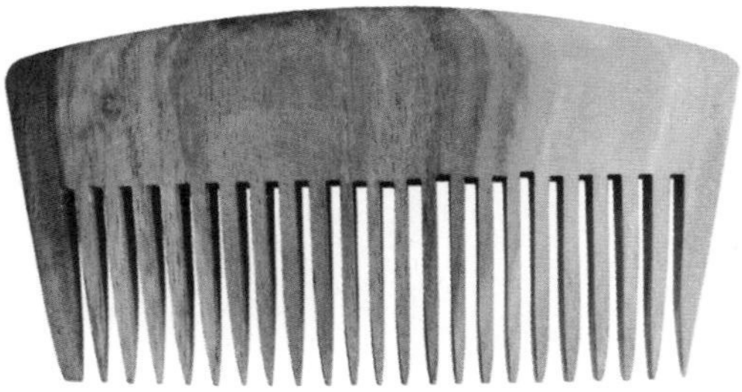

3 Tell those tangles where to go

Fed up with split ends? After you apply conditioner in the shower, slowly run a wide-tooth comb through your hair until all the tangles are out.

4 The weekend off

Feeling lazy? Just can't be bothered to tame that mane? Simple: just pop on a casual cap – preferably one with a straight-talking, voter-friendly slogan. Just watch out for that hat hair, when you take it off.

5 The beach bum

Always keep some sea spray in your fanny pack, for that tousled, just-off-the-beach look.

6 Spray away

You can never use too much hair spray, so squirt on as much as you like and keep your quiff as stiff and strong as American steel.

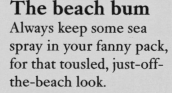

7 Keep your pins in!

Do your bobby pins keep slipping out? Place them on a paper towel and give them a light spray with dry shampoo before inserting them into your hair. No more embarrassing fringe flop!

8 Colour me good!

If you are colouring your hair then remember: warm colours for warm skin tones and cool colours for cool. Orange and blonde? You rock!

TRUMP'S GANG

Stormy Daniels

HAIR:	BLONDE
CUTENESS:	4 cat faces
FAVOURITE COLOUR:	BLONDE
SPARKLE RATING:	4 stars
KINDFULNESS:	63%
POLITICAL STRENGTH:	6/10
FRIENDSHIP FACTOR:	5 hearts

SPECIAL POWER:

STORMY CAN COMMAND THUNDER AND LIGHTNING AT WILL!!

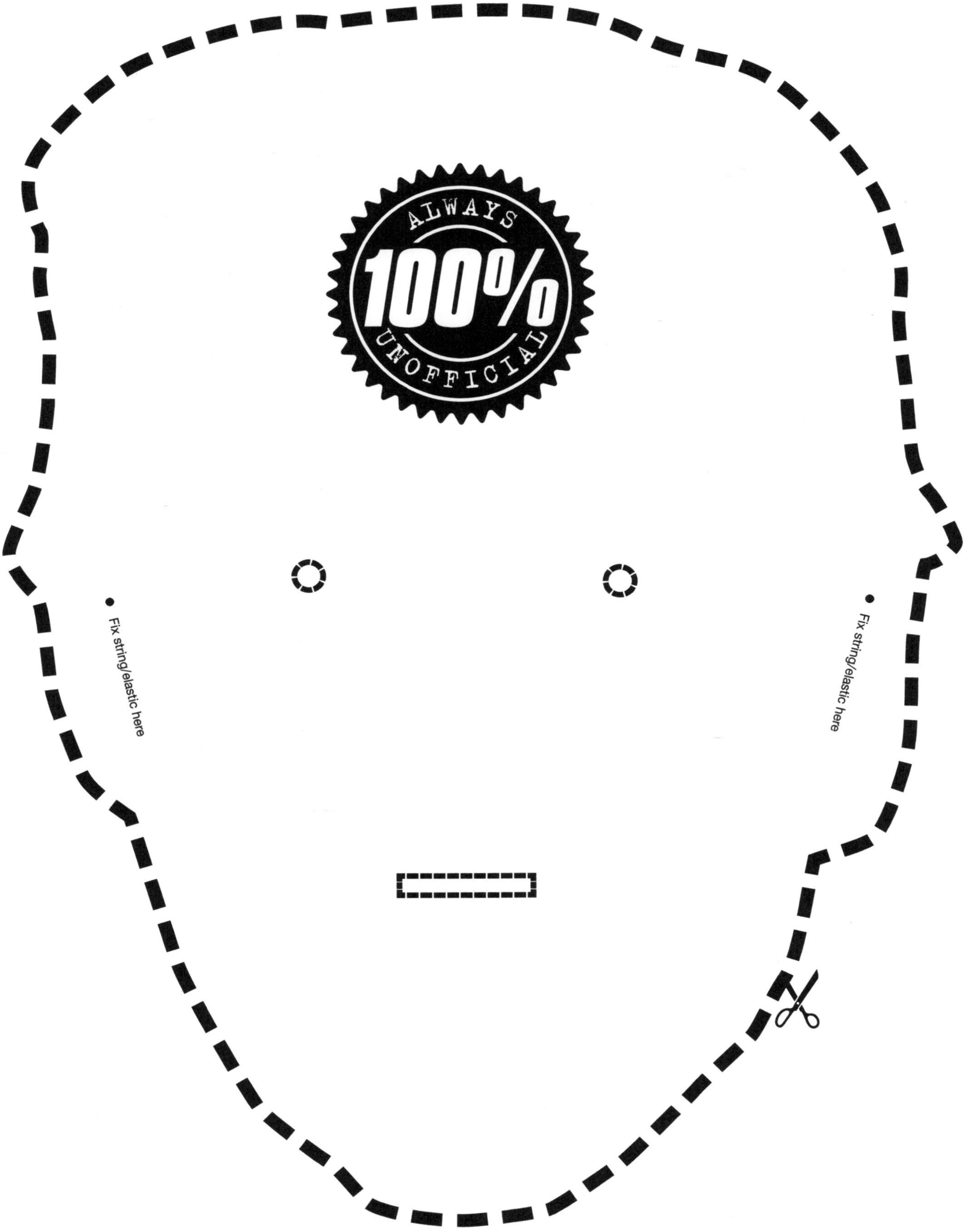

Donald Trump! **FUN MASK**

Donald Trump! FUN MASK

Kim Jong-un! **FUN MASK**

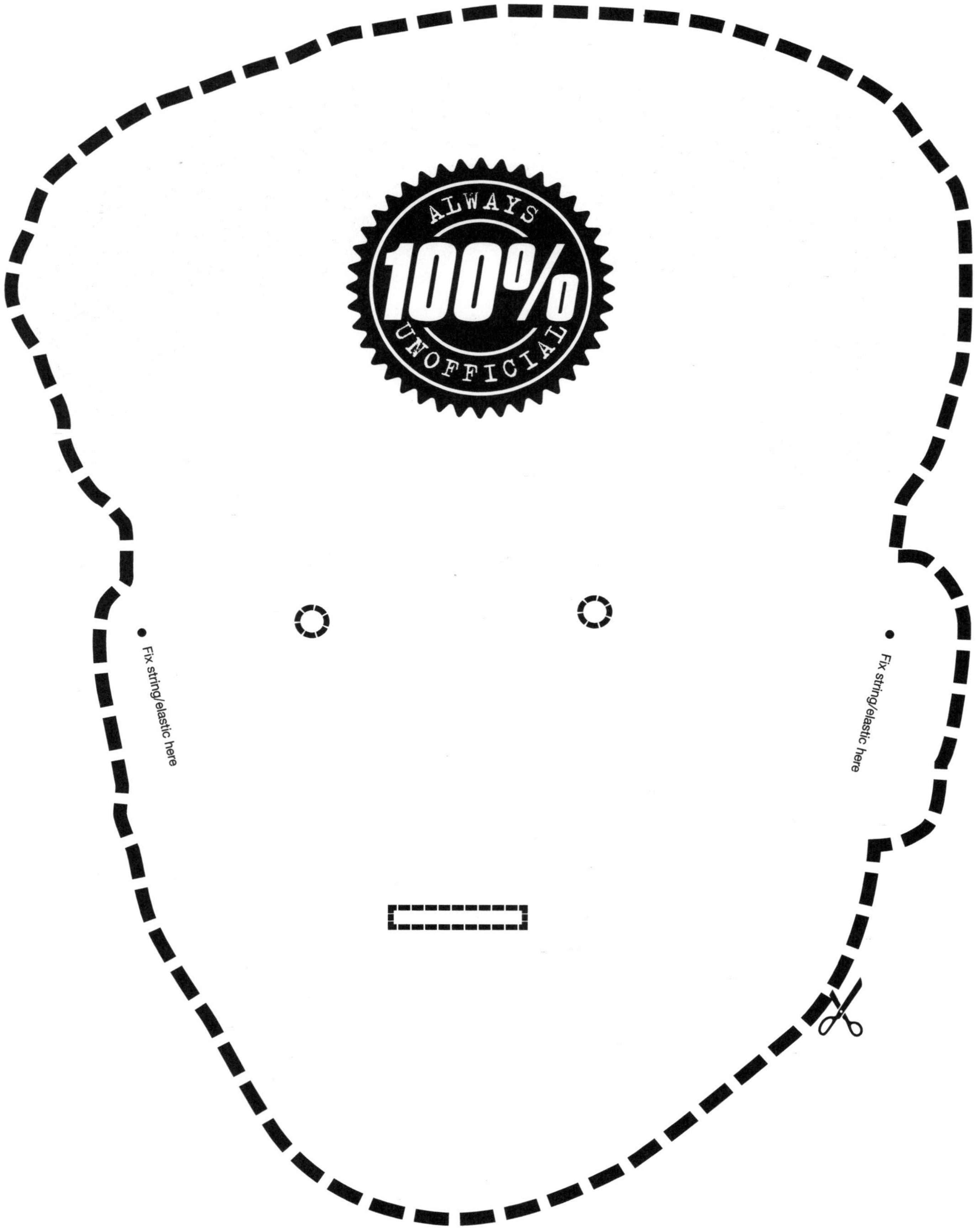

Kim Jong-un! FUN MASK

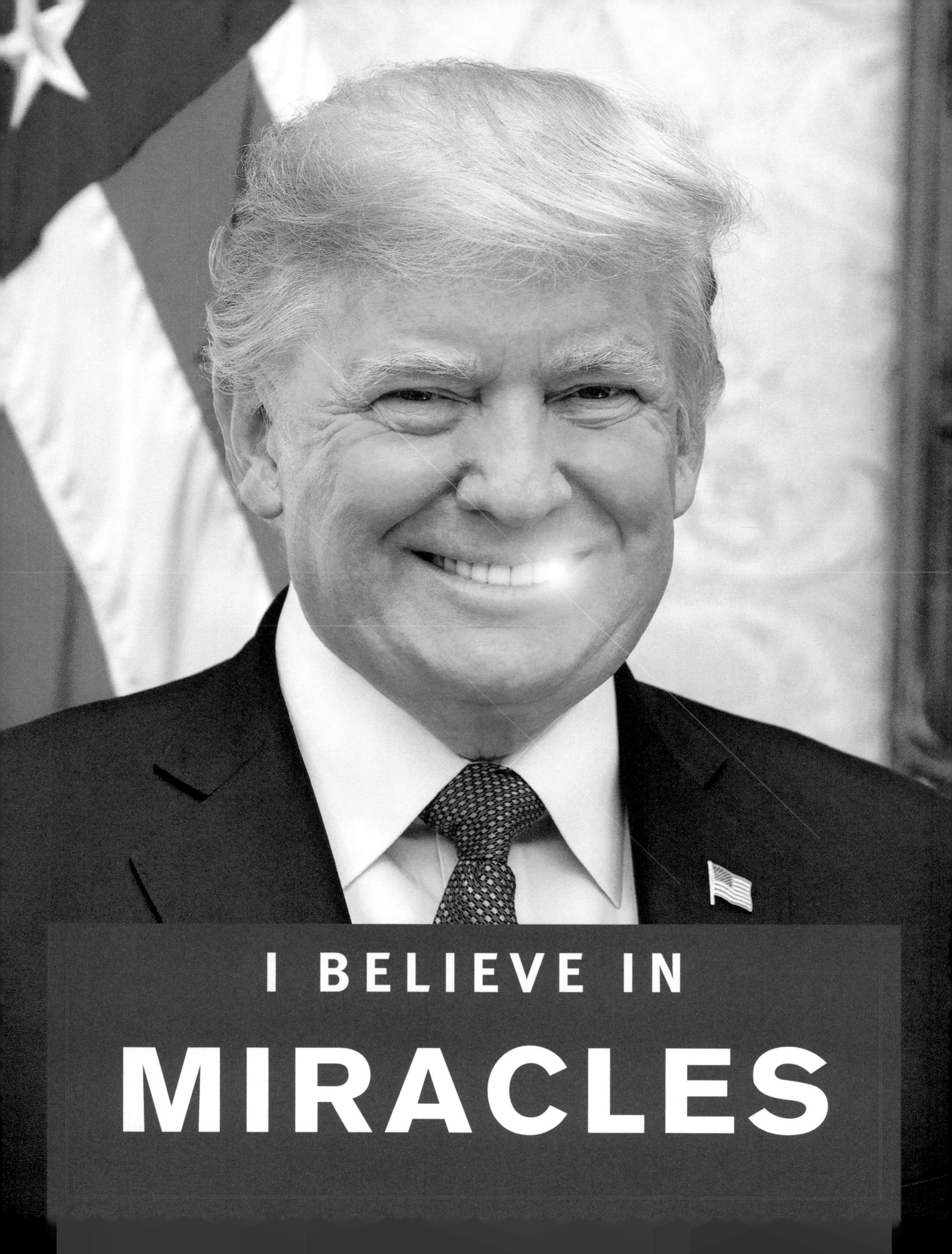
I BELIEVE IN
MIRACLES

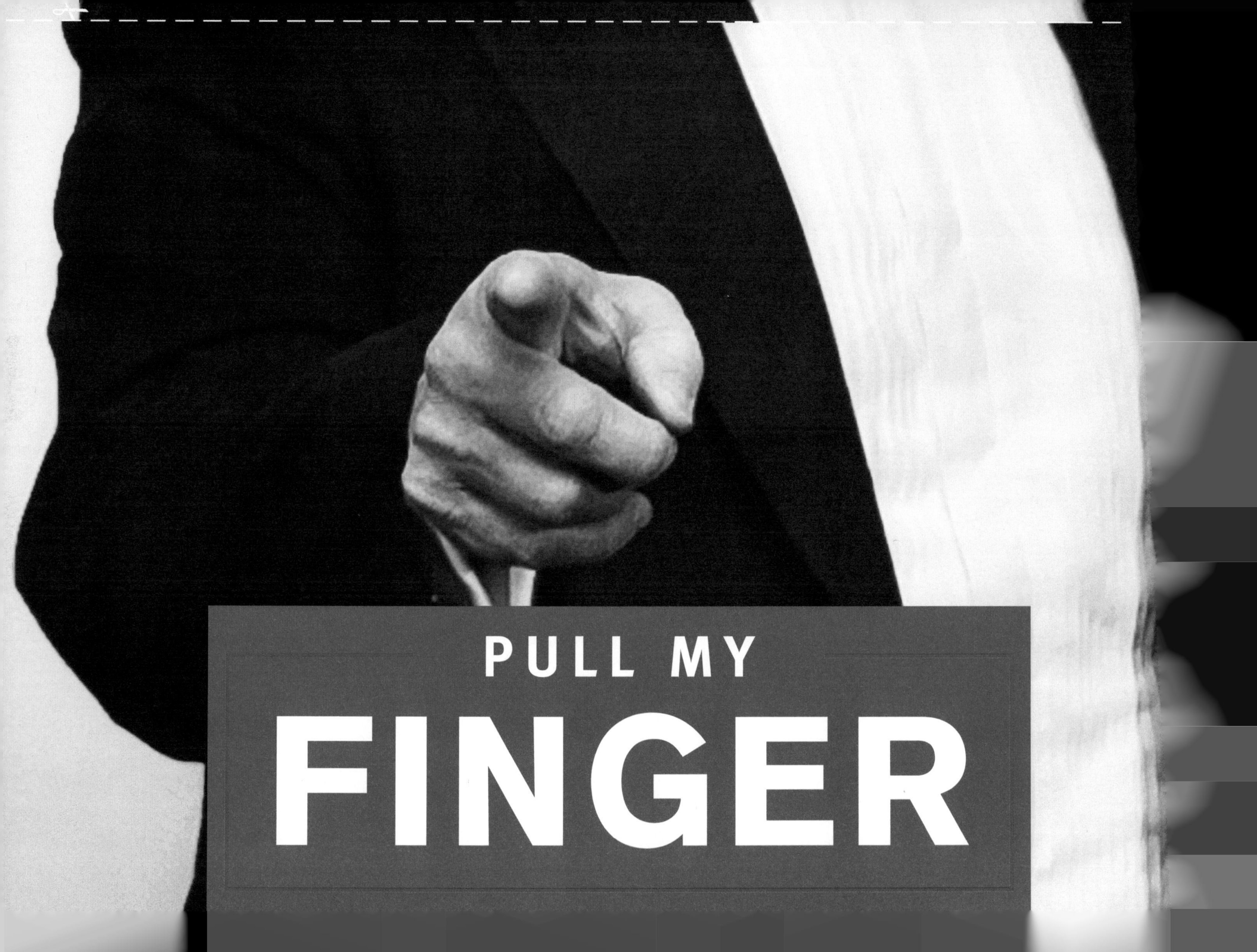

PULL MY FINGER

Don't Stop
Believing!

TRUMP'S GANG

Steve Bannon

HAIR: FLOPPY

CUTENESS: 😻

FAVOURITE COLOUR: BLACK

SPARKLE RATING: – ☆

KINDFULNESS: 6%

POLITICAL STRENGTH: 2/10

FRIENDSHIP FACTOR: N/A

SPECIAL POWER:
STEVE CAN SHOOT FIRE
FROM HIS EYES!!

Face Time with Donald

Everyone has a question for Donald Trump. Unfortunately, he's too busy being a President of the United States / international business icon to answer them directly. So, we have taken your questions and used Donald's tweets to answer them, as if he was really answering you face-to-face.

POCKET MONEY

Q: If you saved up all your pocket money, would you buy a pony, a kitten, a unicorn – or something else, maybe?

Maisie, 8, from Hartlepool

"Got $1.6 Billion to start Wall on Southern Border, rest will be forthcoming. Most importantly, got $700 Billion to rebuild our Military, $716 Billion next year...most ever. Had to waste money on Dem giveaways in order to take care of military pay increase and new equipment."

FAVOURITE FILM

Q: Hello Donald. My favourite film is *Beaches* with Bette Midler. It's so sad! What's your favourite?

Jenny, 38, Debden

"I never liked @BetteMidler's persona or singing and haven't heard her name in years."

HALLOWEEN

Q: If your mum said you could have a Halloween party at your house, what theme would you choose? Vampires or zombies are my favourites!

Lucas, 9, from Basingstoke

"A total WITCH HUNT with massive conflicts of interest!"

Every day is party day for Delicious Donald and

RAPPER QUESTION

Q: If you could ask any famous rapper to rap about just one thing, what would it be?

Carla, 11, West Lothian

"Somebody please inform Jay-Z that because of my policies, Black Unemployment has just been reported to be at the LOWEST RATE EVER RECORDED!"

BATH TIME

Q: Have you ever fallen out with any of your friends? And, if so, why?

Sebastian, 12, Bath

"Why would Kim Jong-un insult me by calling me 'old' when I would NEVER call him 'short and fat'? Oh well, I try so hard to be his friend – and maybe someday that will happen!"

PROUDEST ACHIEVEMENT IN LIFE

Q: What's your proudest achievement in life?

Alaiya, 14, Swansea

"People are proud to be saying Merry Christmas again. I am proud to have led the charge against the assault of our cherished and beautiful phrase.
MERRY CHRISTMAS!!!!!"

BALLET SONG

Q: What's your favourite Spandau Ballet song?

Tony Hadley, 58, London

"So true, thank you."

DONALDS

**IF YOU LOVE DONALD TRUMP,
HERE'S A SELECTION OF OTHER FANTASTIC DONALDS FOR YOU TO ENJOY**

TRUMP JNR

Coincidentally, this 40-year-old debonair Donald has the exact same name as his father (Donald Trump), apart from the 'Jnr' bit. Also coincidentally, Donald Trump (Jnr) has a son with almost exactly the same name, Donald Trump (III) but with no 'Jnr'. And so on.

DUCK

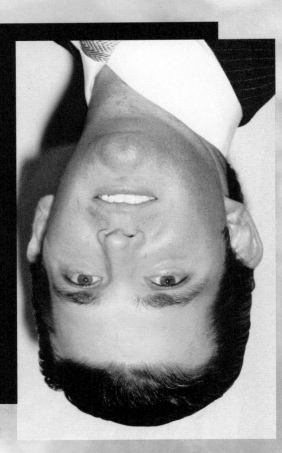

This 84-year-old animated Donald is the life and soul of the cartoon party, but watch out – he can lose his temper quackly (quickly)!

TUSK

Like Donald Trump, Donald Tusk is also a president. But not of America. Sixty-year-old Donald doesn't have real tusks, but he's not too 'long in the tooth' (tusk) to sort out Europe's problems!

Married five times, hunky 68-year-old actor Donald 'Don' Wayne Johnson is best known for playing Detective Crockett and Tubbs in TV's *Miami Vice Machine*. But unlike his other namesake, (D)Wayne Johnson, he's not a rock (The Rock) when it comes to marriage.

JOHNSON

RONALD MC

This 77-year-old (Mc)Donald isn't a real Donald at all – in fact, he's a clown. But Ronald's no clown when it comes to making the world's most successful hamburger: The Big Mac(Donald). Coincidentally, (Mc)Donalds is Donald's (Trump) favourite food.

DONNY'S 'Put a Pin in it' FAKE NEWS BALLOON GAME

Like every red-blooded American Donald LOVES shiny red, white and blue balloons, and like some Americans he HATES fake news! But, oh no! Somebody has mixed up Donald's real balloons with some fake ones. Can you help Donald sort the real news balloons from the fakes? If it's a fake news balloon, then prick it with Donald's fake news pricker.

Donald can fly like a beautiful swan
Trump calls for death penalty for drug traffickers
Donald loves his pony of many colours
25% tariff on foreign steel
White House imposes travel ban from Muslim countries
Donald's limousine turns into a pumpkin after midnight
Donald can lay thousands of tiny golden eggs

DONALD'S PONY CARE TIPS

Every young girl or boy dreams of owning their own pony, and Donald Trump is no different. Looking after a pony is a huge commitment but with a few simple tips from Trump Stables you'll be happily riding off into the sunset on your best friend's powerful back.

WATER BUCKETS

Your pony's water should be checked throughout the day; in the summer it'll need topping up, and in winter you will need to break any ice so he can still drink the water.

STUBBORN DAYS

If your pony has woken up on the wrong side of the hay bale try using an incentive scheme to nudge him in the right direction. Offer him a 'bonus' of carrots or threaten him with redundancy.

LOOK AFTER HIS FEET

Hooves should be picked out every day, regardless of whether they're shod or not.

FOOD AND NUTRITION

For a healthy pony try to remember: Forage, grass and hay, not hamburgers, pizza and cakes.

SHEDDING RAKE

If your pony has been living outside during the winter, a shedding rake will make hair removal easier. Gently rake over the body, avoiding the face and legs. The fine teeth will catch any moulting hair.

SHOW HIM WHO'S THE BOSS

Never allow your pony onto your private jet, however sad he looks. Ponies, international travel and important meetings really don't mix! And whatever you do, don't let him into bed with you!

HAIR CARE

Those flowing locks can become unruly if untended. Brush his mane one hundred times a day and sweep his golden locks over any bald patches that might be forming. Finally use hairspray to hold it all in place.

BUT MOST IMPORTANTLY JUST HAVE FUN WITH YOUR PONY!

And if you get bored, pay somebody else to have fun with your pony for you.

DON'S GONE GOLFIN' GAME

When the pressure gets hot, Donald's not - he just goes golfin'! But what really gets him hot under the collar are pets on the fairway. And greens. In this game, follow Donald's balls around the golf course to see if you can help him get a hole in one – but watch out 'fore' those dogs and cats on the fairway! And greens!

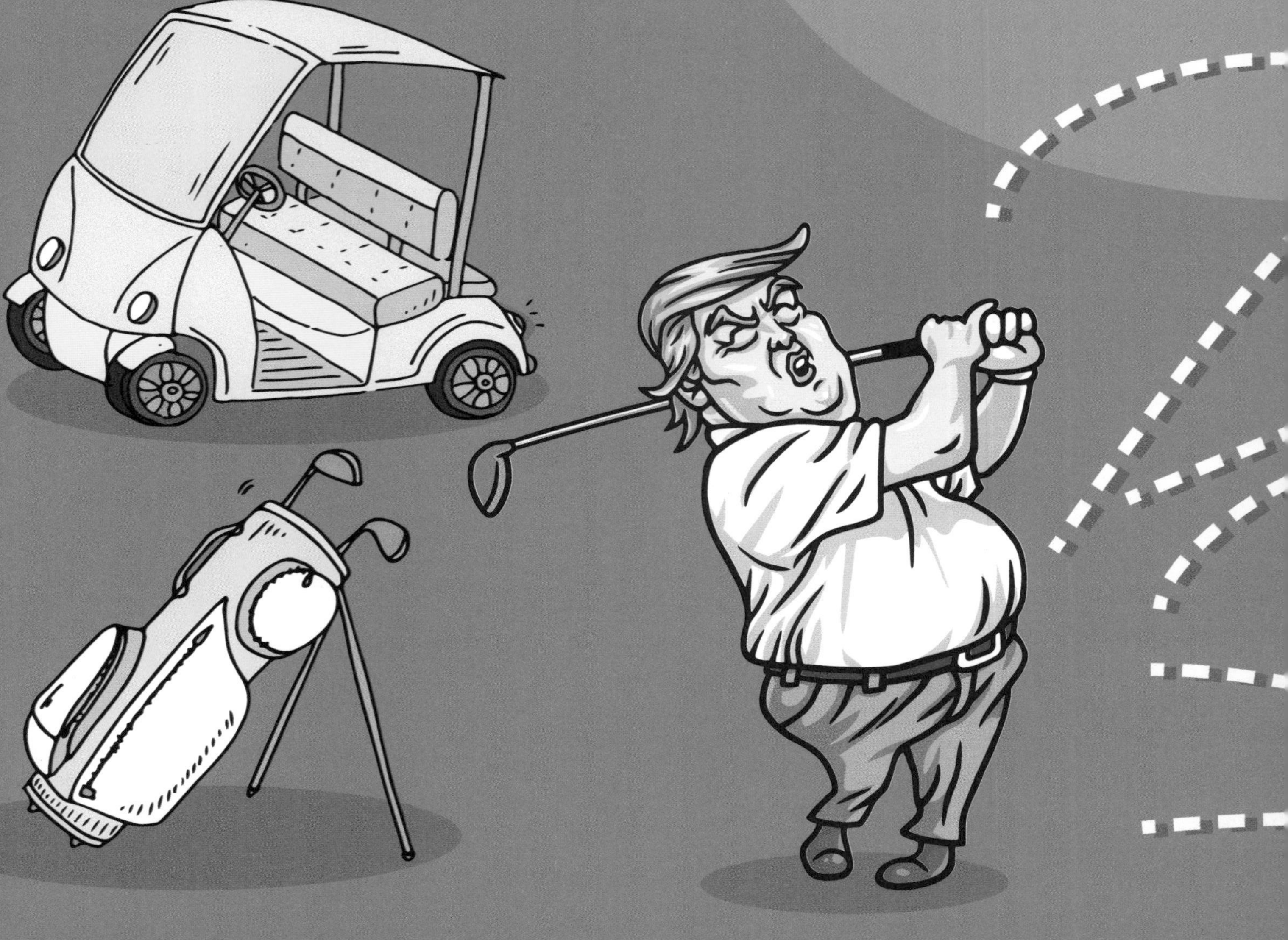

TRUMP LOVE STORY
LINDA HAD A GREAT IDEA FOR BUSINESS BUT LOVE GOT IN THE WAY...
THE APPRENTICE OF LOVE
Starring TV's Francesca Gonshaw from 'Allo 'Allo and Howard's Way as Linda
She thought she was in business, but actually she was in the business of love...
One morning in the 1980s, Linda turned on the radio.
...AND THAT WAS 'I'M TOO SHY SHY' BY POP SENSATIONS KAJAMIGOOGOO. NEXT, WE'LL BE TALKING ABOUT A BIG BUSINESS OPPORTUNITY...
BUSINESS??
Linda fiddled with the radio knob.
I'VE ALWAYS WANTED TO DO BUSINESS BUT NEVER HAD THE OPPORTUNITY. THIS COULD BE MY OPPORTUNITY!
The DJ carried on talking.
...TOP BUSINESS PEOPLE LIKE ALAN SUGAR, DEBORAH MEADEN AND DONALD TRUMP ARE GIVING ADVICE AT A LOCAL BUSINESS FAIR
I CAN'T BELIEVE MY EARS! DISHY DONALD TRUMP!

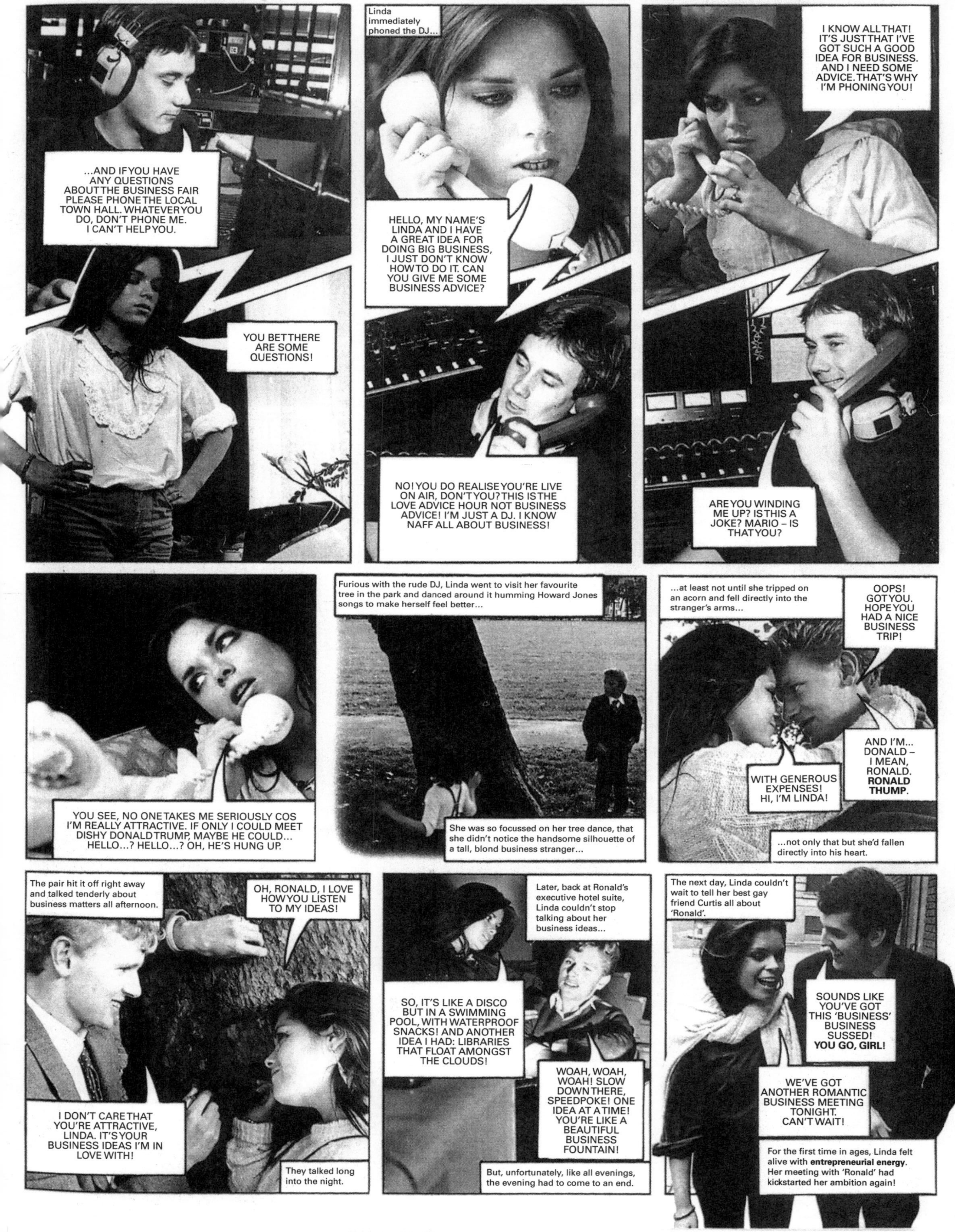
...AND IF YOU HAVE ANY QUESTIONS ABOUT THE BUSINESS FAIR PLEASE PHONE THE LOCAL TOWN HALL. WHATEVER YOU DO, DON'T PHONE ME. I CAN'T HELP YOU.
YOU BET THERE ARE SOME QUESTIONS!
Linda immediately phoned the DJ...
HELLO, MY NAME'S LINDA AND I HAVE A GREAT IDEA FOR DOING BIG BUSINESS, I JUST DON'T KNOW HOW TO DO IT. CAN YOU GIVE ME SOME BUSINESS ADVICE?
NO! YOU DO REALISE YOU'RE LIVE ON AIR, DON'T YOU? THIS IS THE LOVE ADVICE HOUR NOT BUSINESS ADVICE! I'M JUST A DJ. I KNOW NAFF ALL ABOUT BUSINESS!
I KNOW ALL THAT! IT'S JUST THAT I'VE GOT SUCH A GOOD IDEA FOR BUSINESS. AND I NEED SOME ADVICE. THAT'S WHY I'M PHONING YOU!
ARE YOU WINDING ME UP? IS THIS A JOKE? MARIO – IS THAT YOU?
YOU SEE, NO ONE TAKES ME SERIOUSLY COS I'M REALLY ATTRACTIVE. IF ONLY I COULD MEET DISHY DONALD TRUMP, MAYBE HE COULD... HELLO...? HELLO...? OH, HE'S HUNG UP.
Furious with the rude DJ, Linda went to visit her favourite tree in the park and danced around it humming Howard Jones songs to make herself feel better...
She was so focussed on her tree dance, that she didn't notice the handsome silhouette of a tall, blond business stranger...
...at least not until she tripped on an acorn and fell directly into the stranger's arms...
OOPS! GOT YOU. HOPE YOU HAD A NICE BUSINESS TRIP!
WITH GENEROUS EXPENSES! HI, I'M LINDA!
AND I'M... DONALD – I MEAN, RONALD. **RONALD THUMP**.
...not only that but she'd fallen directly into his heart.
The pair hit it off right away and talked tenderly about business matters all afternoon.
OH, RONALD, I LOVE HOW YOU LISTEN TO MY IDEAS!
I DON'T CARE THAT YOU'RE ATTRACTIVE, LINDA. IT'S YOUR BUSINESS IDEAS I'M IN LOVE WITH!
They talked long into the night.
Later, back at Ronald's executive hotel suite, Linda couldn't stop talking about her business ideas...
SO, IT'S LIKE A DISCO BUT IN A SWIMMING POOL, WITH WATERPROOF SNACKS! AND ANOTHER IDEA I HAD: LIBRARIES THAT FLOAT AMONGST THE CLOUDS!
WOAH, WOAH, WOAH! SLOW DOWN THERE, SPEEDPOKE! ONE IDEA AT A TIME! YOU'RE LIKE A BEAUTIFUL BUSINESS FOUNTAIN!
But, unfortunately, like all evenings, the evening had to come to an end.
The next day, Linda couldn't wait to tell her best gay friend Curtis all about 'Ronald'.
SOUNDS LIKE YOU'VE GOT THIS 'BUSINESS' BUSINESS SUSSED! **YOU GO, GIRL!**
WE'VE GOT ANOTHER ROMANTIC BUSINESS MEETING TONIGHT. CAN'T WAIT!
For the first time in ages, Linda felt alive with **entrepreneurial energy**. Her meeting with 'Ronald' had kickstarted her ambition again!

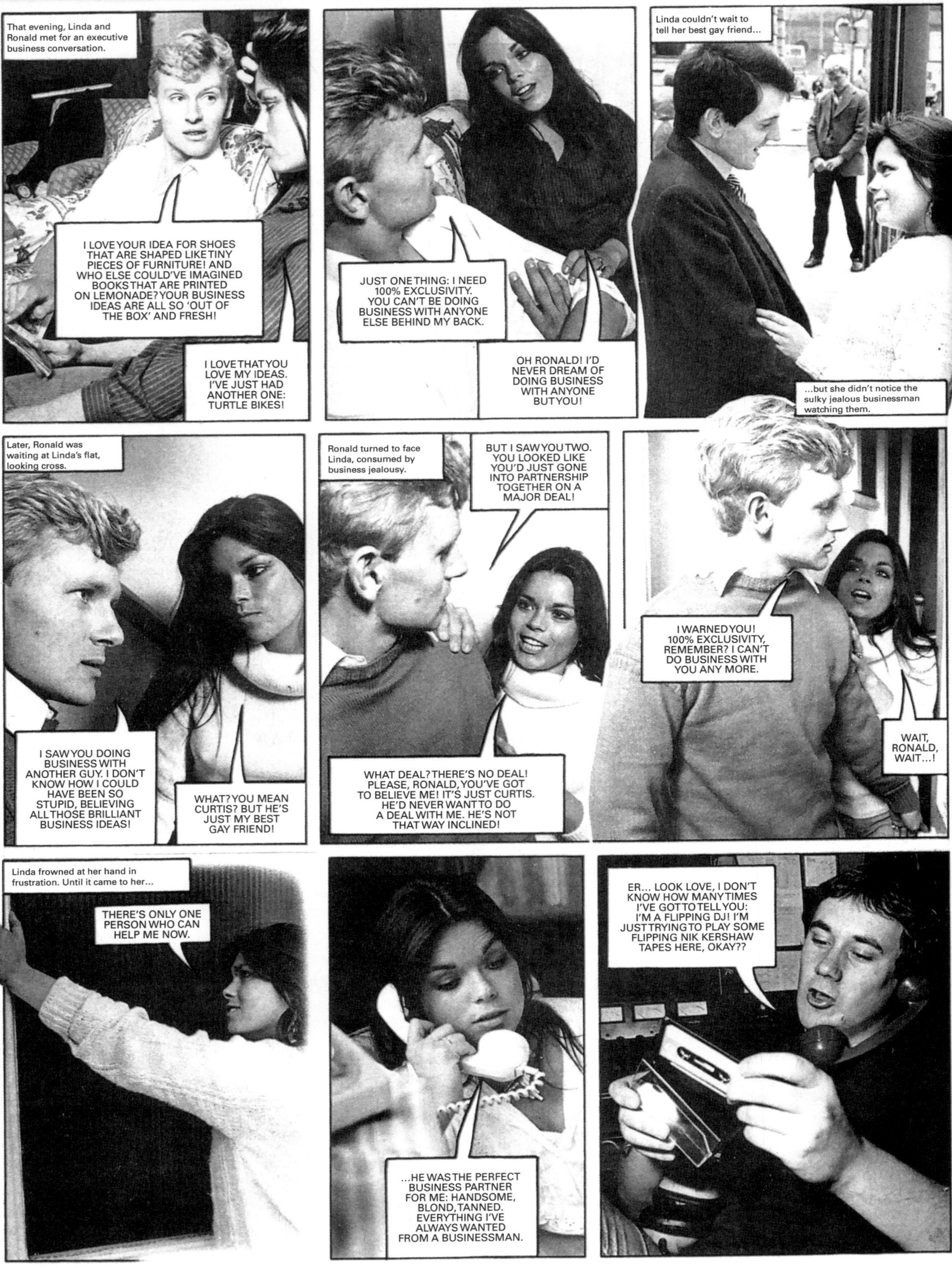
That evening, Linda and Ronald met for an executive business conversation.
I LOVE YOUR IDEA FOR SHOES THAT ARE SHAPED LIKE TINY PIECES OF FURNITURE! AND WHO ELSE COULD'VE IMAGINED BOOKS THAT ARE PRINTED ON LEMONADE? YOUR BUSINESS IDEAS ARE ALL SO 'OUT OF THE BOX' AND FRESH!
I LOVE THAT YOU LOVE MY IDEAS. I'VE JUST HAD ANOTHER ONE: TURTLE BIKES!
JUST ONE THING: I NEED 100% EXCLUSIVITY. YOU CAN'T BE DOING BUSINESS WITH ANYONE ELSE BEHIND MY BACK.
OH RONALD! I'D NEVER DREAM OF DOING BUSINESS WITH ANYONE BUT YOU!
Linda couldn't wait to tell her best gay friend...
...but she didn't notice the sulky jealous businessman watching them.
Later, Ronald was waiting at Linda's flat, looking cross.
I SAW YOU DOING BUSINESS WITH ANOTHER GUY. I DON'T KNOW HOW I COULD HAVE BEEN SO STUPID, BELIEVING ALL THOSE BRILLIANT BUSINESS IDEAS!
WHAT? YOU MEAN CURTIS? BUT HE'S JUST MY BEST GAY FRIEND!
Ronald turned to face Linda, consumed by business jealousy.
BUT I SAW YOU TWO. YOU LOOKED LIKE YOU'D JUST GONE INTO PARTNERSHIP TOGETHER ON A MAJOR DEAL!
WHAT DEAL? THERE'S NO DEAL! PLEASE, RONALD, YOU'VE GOT TO BELIEVE ME! IT'S JUST CURTIS. HE'D NEVER WANT TO DO A DEAL WITH ME. HE'S NOT THAT WAY INCLINED!
I WARNED YOU! 100% EXCLUSIVITY, REMEMBER? I CAN'T DO BUSINESS WITH YOU ANY MORE.
WAIT, RONALD, WAIT...!
Linda frowned at her hand in frustration. Until it came to her...
THERE'S ONLY ONE PERSON WHO CAN HELP ME NOW.
...HE WAS THE PERFECT BUSINESS PARTNER FOR ME: HANDSOME, BLOND, TANNED. EVERYTHING I'VE ALWAYS WANTED FROM A BUSINESSMAN.
ER... LOOK LOVE, I DON'T KNOW HOW MANY TIMES I'VE GOT TO TELL YOU: I'M A FLIPPING DJ! I'M JUST TRYING TO PLAY SOME FLIPPING NIK KERSHAW TAPES HERE, OKAY??

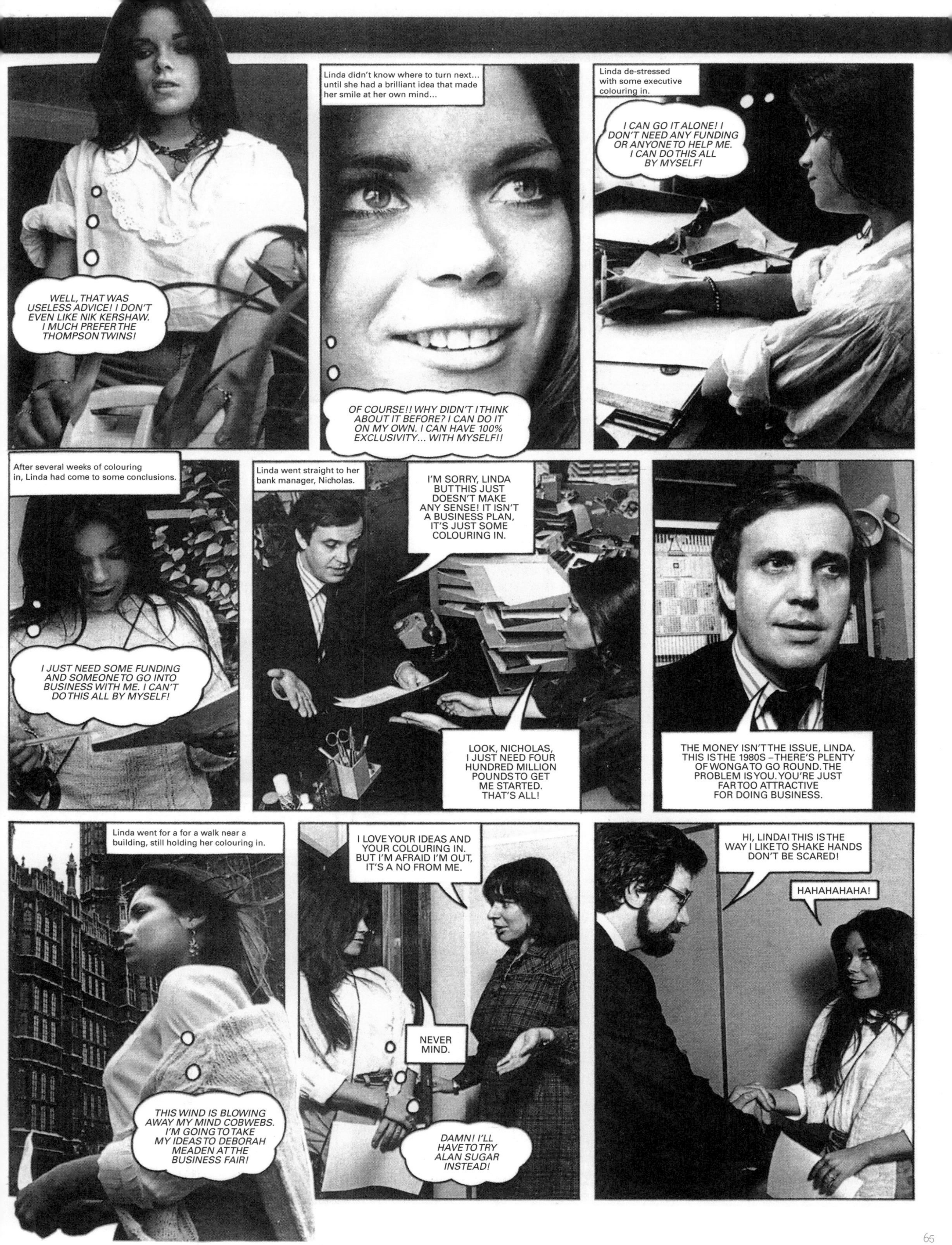

WELL, THAT WAS USELESS ADVICE! I DON'T EVEN LIKE NIK KERSHAW. I MUCH PREFER THE THOMPSON TWINS!
Linda didn't know where to turn next... until she had a brilliant idea that made her smile at her own mind...
OF COURSE!! WHY DIDN'T I THINK ABOUT IT BEFORE? I CAN DO IT ON MY OWN. I CAN HAVE 100% EXCLUSIVITY... WITH MYSELF!!
Linda de-stressed with some executive colouring in.
I CAN GO IT ALONE! I DON'T NEED ANY FUNDING OR ANYONE TO HELP ME. I CAN DO THIS ALL BY MYSELF!
After several weeks of colouring in, Linda had come to some conclusions.
I JUST NEED SOME FUNDING AND SOMEONE TO GO INTO BUSINESS WITH ME. I CAN'T DO THIS ALL BY MYSELF!
Linda went straight to her bank manager, Nicholas.
I'M SORRY, LINDA BUT THIS JUST DOESN'T MAKE ANY SENSE! IT ISN'T A BUSINESS PLAN, IT'S JUST SOME COLOURING IN.
LOOK, NICHOLAS, I JUST NEED FOUR HUNDRED MILLION POUNDS TO GET ME STARTED. THAT'S ALL!
THE MONEY ISN'T THE ISSUE, LINDA. THIS IS THE 1980S – THERE'S PLENTY OF WONGA TO GO ROUND. THE PROBLEM IS YOU. YOU'RE JUST FAR TOO ATTRACTIVE FOR DOING BUSINESS.
Linda went for a for a walk near a building, still holding her colouring in.
THIS WIND IS BLOWING AWAY MY MIND COBWEBS. I'M GOING TO TAKE MY IDEAS TO DEBORAH MEADEN AT THE BUSINESS FAIR!
I LOVE YOUR IDEAS AND YOUR COLOURING IN. BUT I'M AFRAID I'M OUT, IT'S A NO FROM ME.
NEVER MIND.
DAMN! I'LL HAVE TO TRY ALAN SUGAR INSTEAD!
HI, LINDA! THIS IS THE WAY I LIKE TO SHAKE HANDS DON'T BE SCARED!
HAHAHAHAHA!

Once the handshakes were over, Linda and Alan sat down to talk big business.
WOW, THIS IS GREAT, LINDA. AND YOU ONLY NEED FOUR HUNDRED MILLION POUNDS, YOU SAY? THAT'S PEANUTS TO ME. SO TELL ME MORE ABOUT YOUR JAZZ CURTAINS AND YOUR TORTOISE BOAT.
IT'S A TURTLE BIKE, ACTUALLY. ARE YOU EVEN LISTENING?
NO – AND THAT'S THE PROBLEM. DON'T YOU SEE, LINDA? YOU'RE JUST WAY TOO ATTRACTIVE TO DO BUSINESS. SO, WITH REGRET – YOU'RE FIRED!
B-BUT... YOU HAVEN'T EVEN HIRED ME YET!
Alone and too attractive for business, Linda returned to her tree. But instead of dancing, she hummed a sad tune.
"WHAT IS LO-O-O-OVE ANYWAY, DOES ANYBODY LOVE ANYBODY ANYWAY, WHAT IS LO-O-O-OVE ANYWAY, DOES ANYBODY LOVE ANYBODY ANYWAY, HMMMM-HMMMMM HM-MMM-HMMM"
But she wasn't alone.
WHAT ARE YOU DOING HERE? I-I THOUGHT...
I HAD TO COME, LINDA. I HEARD SOMEONE HUMMING HOWARD JONES IN THEIR MIND AND KNEW IT WOULD BE YOU.
BUT- BUT... I THOUGHT WE WEREN'T BUSINESS PARTNERS ANY MORE! I THOUGHT YOU'D GONE TO CHINA!
I SAW YOUR BEST GAY FRIEND CURTIS IN A GAY BAR AND REALISED HE'S A GAY MAN, NOT A BUSINESSMAN. ALSO, I PICKED UP YOUR COLOURING IN FROM ALAN SUGAR. IT'S GREAT!
DO YOU REALLY MEAN IT? IT TOOK ME WEEKS! I TRIED NOT TO GO OVER EDGES, BUT IT'S JUST SO FLIPPING HARD. I'M SO PLEASED YOU HEARD ME HUMMING, RONALD.
I'M AFRAID I HAVEN'T BEEN 110% HONEST WITH YOU, LINDA. MY NAME ISN'T RONALD THUMP... I'M ACTUALLY **DONALD TRUMP**, THE FAMOUS AMERICAN BUSINESS TYCOON AND FUTURE PRESIDENT OF THE UNITED STATES!
WHY DID YOU LIE TO ME? I KNEW IT! I KNEW THERE WAS SOMETHING DISHY ABOUT YOU!
I COULDN'T GET YOUR BRILLIANT BUSINESS IDEAS OUT OF MY HEAD. ESPECIALLY THE SPONGE NECKLACES AND THE CHOCOLATE RADARS. GENIUS! ...AND IT JUST SO HAPPENS I'VE GOT A SPARE FOUR HUNDRED MILLION POUNDS WITH **YOUR NAME** ON!
YOU HAD ME AT FOUR HUNDRED MILLION POUNDS. DONALD TRUMP – WOULD YOU DO ME THE HONOUR OF DOING BUSINESS WITH ME?
THE END

A A A B B B C C C

D D D E E E F F F G

G G H H H I I I J J

J K K K L L L M M

M N N N O O O P

P P Q Q Q R R R S

S S T T T U U U V

V V W W W X X

X Y Y Y Z Z Z

MAKE 'EVERYTHING' GREAT AGAIN!!

Donald Trump, like Presidents Ronald Reagan and Bill Clinton before him, wants to "Make America Great Again". But what about you, what do you want to make great? Perhaps you want Daddy to be great again. Or ponies. Or maybe you'd just like your own town to be great again. Using the letters on the previous page cut out and spell what YOU want to be great again. Now, using sticky tape or glitter glue, insert the word into the Donald-endorsed banner on the next page.

NOW WE CAN ALL BE GREAT AGAIN!

MAKE

GREAT AGAIN

SHERIFF TRUMP

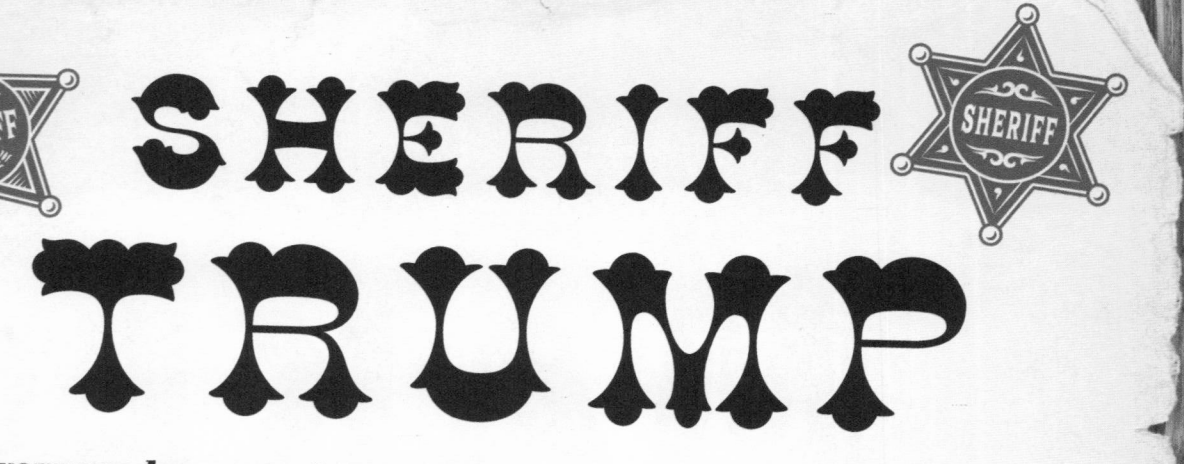

Everyone loves cowboys and everyone loves Donald Trump –

NOW YOU CAN HAVE BOTH!

Sheriff Trump is the fastest President in the West and he always gets his man. Deputy Pence has accidentally locked himself in the cells again, now YOU are his deputy. Fill out the fun cowboy facts about yourself below to create your very own cowboy character!

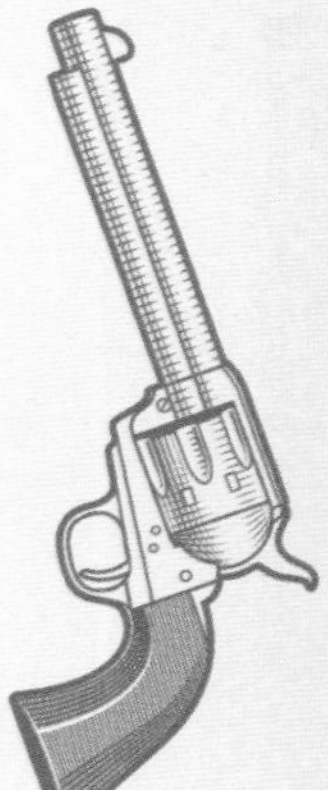

My cowboy name is:

....

My horse is called:

....

Sheriff Trump is my favourite cowboy because:

....

....

My favourite cowboy drink is:

....

My cowboy politics are:

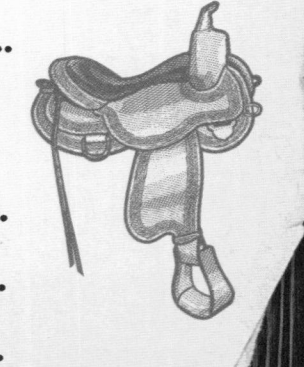

....

....

....

In the blank space below, draw a picture of SHERIFF TRUMP, then draw yourself beside him, as Sheriff Trump's trusty deputy!

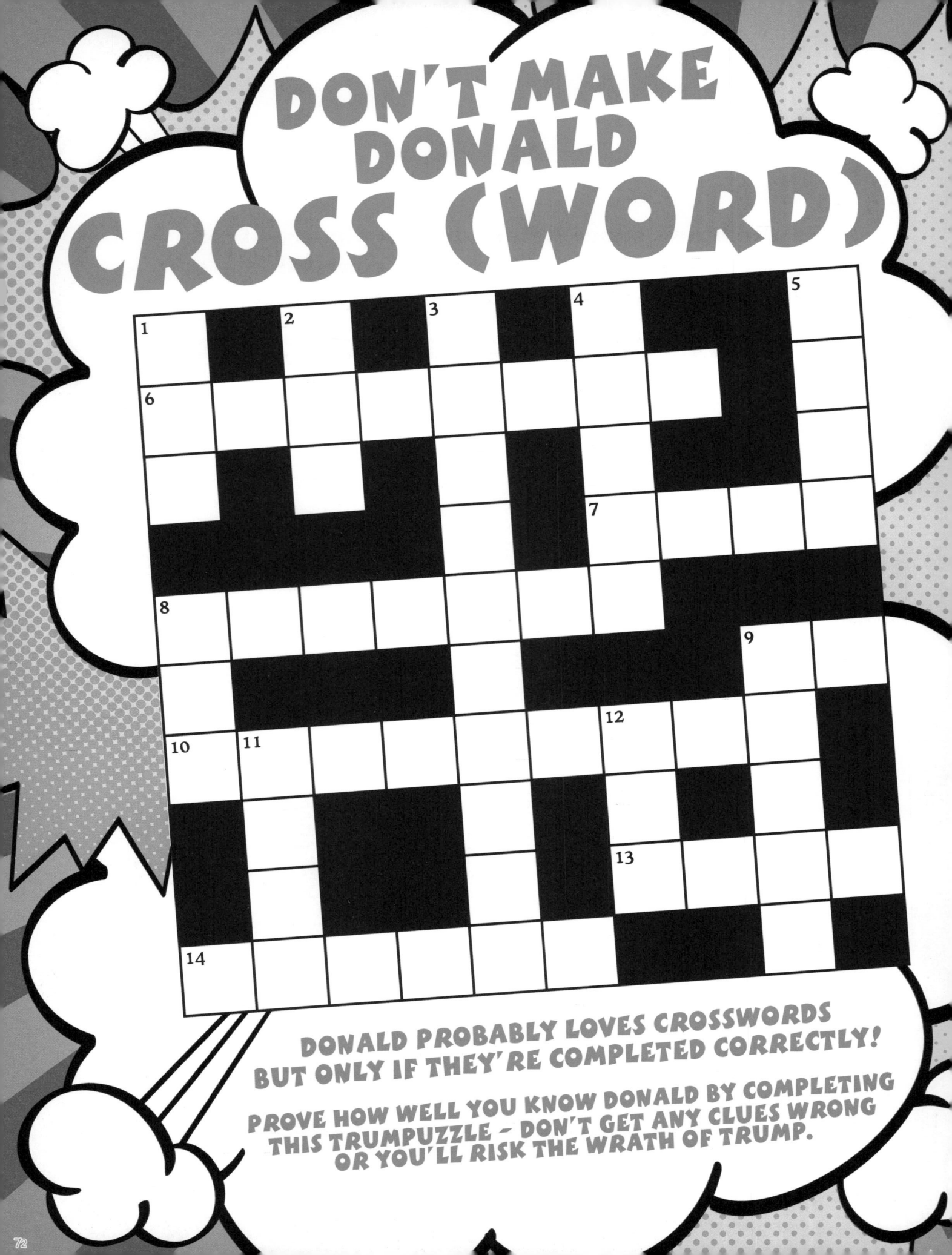

DON'T MAKE DONALD CROSS (WORD)

DONALD PROBABLY LOVES CROSSWORDS BUT ONLY IF THEY'RE COMPLETED CORRECTLY!

PROVE HOW WELL YOU KNOW DONALD BY COMPLETING THIS TRUMPUZZLE – DON'T GET ANY CLUES WRONG OR YOU'LL RISK THE WRATH OF TRUMP.

ACROSS

6. A so, so big beauty pageant owned by Donald until 2015, Miss _ _ _ _ _ _ _ _ (8)
7. What Donald's grandfather might call a German super hero, man (4)
8. Donald's last word if he were Charles Foster Kane (7)
9. Donald's favourite word that he uses to such a great extent (2)
10. Donald's current position (9)
13. Business arrangement agreed on by Donald and other party (4)
14. Borough of New York that Donald was born in (6)

DOWN

1. Donald is a _ _ _ loving president (3)
2. A civilian foreign intelligence service of the United States federal government, tasked with gathering, processing, and analyzing national security information from around the world, primarily through the use of human intelligence (3)
3. Donald's political party (10)
4. Someone who pretends to be something they're not to Donald (5)
5. Salutation you might use at the beginning of a letter you might send to Donald (4)
8. If Donald were a Hip-hop artist he might do this instead of talking (3)
9. Meaty Trump business from 2007 (5)
11. A Hindu demon who swallows the sun, causing eclipses that Donald might have heard of (4)
12. A Muslim religious festival marking the end of Ramadan that Donald might celebrate (3)

TRUMP'S GANG

Barack Obama

HAIR:	GREY
CUTENESS:	😻😻😻
FAVOURITE COLOUR:	SAFFRON
SPARKLE RATING:	☆☆☆☆
KINDFULNESS:	88%
POLITICAL STRENGTH:	8/10
FRIENDSHIP FACTOR:	♥

SPECIAL POWER:
BARACK CAN FLY LIKE AN EAGLE!!

The SPEEDING PHANTOM

A Locker Room Gang Mystery

By Thaniel Waymoore

"Gee wiz!" said Cecilia, looking up at the clear spring sky. "It sure is a beautiful day for an adventure."

"It sure is, Cissy," agreed Mary, her sensible older sister.

"Mew!" said Kitty, their faithful feline companion, as if to say, "I agree!" Kitty followed the sisters on all their adventures. The O'Henry girls came from the poor side of town but today they were venturing into the most prosperous part of the city to visit their rich cousin, Bernadette, for tea and English muffins.

But just as they were about to cross the road, a large expensive-looking car came screeching around the corner and hurtled towards them.

"Cissy, look out!" cried Mary, pulling her sister out of the way.

"Meeee-eeew!" mewed Kitty, as if to say, "You madman!"

"You're a madman!" shouted Mary, shaking her fist at the driver of the vehicle as it sped off into the distance.

"Golly gosh! That was close. Did you get the licence plate?" asked Cecilia.

"No," said Mary. "The driver was going much too fast. All I saw was that he had a shock of magnificent strawberry-blond hair.

"Mew! Mew!" said Kitty urgently, as if to say, "I've found a clue!"

"Wait – I think Kitty has found a clue," said Cecilia.

"Tyre marks," said Mary. "And not just any tyre marks. These come from a 2015 Rolls-Royce Phantom. There's only one person rich enough to drive one of those. And he lives at the very top of that tall, shiny tower. Come on, Cissy. Let's investigate."

"But what about tea with our cousin?" asked Cecilia.

"Bernadette's muffins can wait," said Mary. "The Locker Room Gang has a mystery to solve!"

When they reached the tall, gleaming tower, the brave girls entered the lobby and tried to look inconspicuous amongst all the rich business people who lived and worked there.

"We need to find a way to sneak past security and get up to the penthouse to look for more clues," said Mary.

But it was too late – the girls had been spotted! And before they knew what was happening, a team of crack security guards had taken them all the way up to the top of the tower and marched them down a long, expensive-looking corridor to a large, opulent door.

The door opened into a vast golden-coloured room filled with the most extravagant treasures anyone could possibly imagine. At the far end of the room stood a man in an expensive business suit with his back to them.

"We caught these two poor kids and their cat sniffing around in the lobby," said a security guard.

The man turned around.

"Mary, look! Magnificent strawberry-blond hair!" whispered Cecilia.

"I own this tower and you girls are in big, big trouble. Very big trouble," said the man.

"No, sir – you're in trouble," said Cecilia, bravely. The man couldn't hide his surprise, his sandy eyebrows rising high on his naturally tanned forehead.

"You own a 2015 Rolls-Royce Phantom, do you not?" asked Mary.

"Yes, I do," said the man. "Except last Thursday… it was stolen."

"Stolen? Wait. So, it couldn't have been you who nearly knocked us down this morning, then," said Cecilia.

"No. And not only that, but ever since then, the fake news media has been reporting all kinds of fake news stories about me carrying out crimes, such as extramarital affairs with adult film stars, collusion with foreign heads of state and tax evasion."

"Mew!" said Kitty, as if to say, "I hate fake news!"

"Hmmm," said Mary thoughtfully. "It's almost as if there's an imposter going around trying to get you into trouble, Mr…?"

"Call me Donald," said the kindly, wise tycoon.

"This sounds like a case for the Locker Room Gang!" said Cecilia.

So, with the friendly, generous magnate's blessing, the girls set to work looking for clues all around the elaborately decorated apartment. It wasn't long before Kitty began mewing excitedly.

"Kitty has found another clue," exclaimed Cecilia. It was a single strand of strawberry-blond hair.

"Wait," said Mary. "This isn't human hair. It's horsehair, see?" Sure enough, the hair felt coarse to the touch.

"Gee, you're right," said Cecilia, "Just like in our previous adventure – the George Bush Horsehair Affair. This horsehair has come from a wig!"

"But these quarters are where my faithful manservant Jenkins lives," said their host.

"Where exactly is Jenkins?" asked Mary.

"Well, that's the funny thing," said the tall, benevolent businessman. "Jenkins has been missing since–"

"Thursday?" said Mary, cutting him off.

"Exactly," said the stable genius. "How on Earth did you know?"

"No time to explain," said Mary. "But don't worry, I have a plan."

And so, clever Mary laid a trap for the imposter, by putting a pair of Donald's finest diamond-encrusted golf balls on display in the tower's lobby and telling the compassionate entrepreneur

to tweet about it, inviting all the world to come and see them.

"This imposter, whoever he is, will be unable to resist the temptation to try and steal a pair of Donald's jewelled golf balls," said Mary.

Later that night, Mary, Cecilia, Kitty and Donald hid behind the concierge's desk and waited. The glistening balls had already attracted a lot of attention, but now the crowds were dying down.

"Look," whispered Cecilia, pointing to a figure who had entered the lobby.

"It can't be," said Donald. "It's… me!"

The other Donald made his way to where the sparkling balls sat on their satin display cushion. He checked that nobody was looking, then took the balls and slipped them into a small sack. Just then, the girls leapt out and caught the thief red-handed.

"Stop – in the name of the Locker Room Gang!" said Mary.

"Dagnabbit! You caught me!" said the other Donald.

"It's like staring into a mirror," said Donald.

"That's just a disguise," said Cecilia, pulling off the thief's strawberry-blond horsehair wig.

"Jenkins, my manservant!" exclaimed Donald.

"That's also just a disguise," said Mary, pulling off another wig. Underneath was none other than Hillary Clinton.

"Yes, it was me all along," said Hillary Clinton. "You stole my political future, Donald, so I wanted to steal something away from you – your reputation."

"We'll take those back, thank you very much," said Cecilia, seizing the small sack of balls.

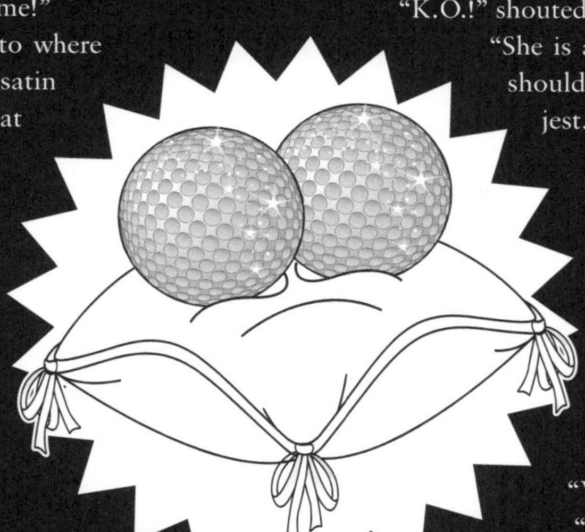

Suddenly, in the blink of an eye, Hillary Clinton snatched Kitty and held a gun to her head.

"Meeew!" said Kitty, as if to say, "Help! She's holding a gun to my head!"

"One move and the cat gets it," said the evil Democrat.

But she hadn't seen Donald creeping up behind her with an expensive, tasteful ornament, which he smashed over Hillary's head. Kitty leapt safely out of her hands as the bitter, twisted politician fell to the ground, unconscious.

"K.O.!" shouted Mary, punching the air.

"She is a nasty, nasty woman," said Donald. "You should never grab a pussy like that – not even in jest."

"I believe these are yours," said Cecilia, handing Donald his balls back.

"I don't know how to thank you girls," said the altruistic capitalist. "But I wonder if we could keep all of this to ourselves. It could be so, so awkward for me if the fake news media got wind of what happened here today."

"Don't worry, Donald," said Cecilia. "We're the Locker Room Gang…"

"…And what happens in the locker room stays in the locker room," said Mary.

"Mew!" said Kitty, and everyone laughed.

The End

ANSWERS

Donald Word Search

Q	S	Y	A	I	S	S	U	R	B	H	A	I	R
U	E	S	T	A	T	E	A	R	N	O	C	L	N
E	C	Z	M	I	S	B	G	Z	I	T	V	K	S
E	I	Z	C	B	S	L	O	C	K	E	R	C	N
N	T	T	M	S	P	R	V	J	F	L	O	G	O
S	N	L	S	I	A	M	E	L	A	N	I	A	I
N	E	Q	A	F	L	J	U	V	B	V	Y	Y	L
A	R	O	O	M	G	L	Z	R	I	G	H	T	L
M	P	E	N	C	E	S	I	T	V	N	E	C	I
R	P	E	N	O	L	A	E	O	A	K	U	S	B
E	A	E	R	O	K	J	K	O	N	I	S	A	C
G	E	M	N	S	E	M	O	H	A	L	R	A	M

Trumpunzel's Trumpuzzle

Follow the middle strand of hair to hop up Trump Tower and awaken your sleeping Prince with a tender kiss.

ANSWERS

Don't Make Donald Cross(word)

F		C		R		P			D
U	N	I	V	E	R	S	E		E
N		A		P		E			A
				U		U	B	E	R
R	O	S	E	B	U	D			
A				L				S	O
P	R	E	S	I	D	E	N	T	
	A			C		I		E	
	H			A		D	E	A	L
Q	U	E	E	N	S			K	

Don's Gone Golfin' Game

Follow the course of the third from the bottoms golf ball to score a hole in one.

ALWAYS 100% UNOFFICIAL

Photo Credits

Alamy.com: page 18, Splash News; page 23, Pictorial Press Ltd; page 26, White House Photo; page 36, Francis Specker; page 37, Xinhua; page 39, IanDagnall Computing; page 40, ZUMA Press, Inc.; page 43, Enrique Shore; page 69, ZUMA Press, Inc.

Shutterstock.com: page 7, a katz; page 13, Free Wind 2014; page 16, a katz; page 29, Evan El-Amin; page 32 (bottom right), Albert H. Teich; page 33 (top right), Joseph Sohm; page 33 (bottom right), a katz; page 34, Tinseltown; page 42, Evan El-Amin; page 44 (top), a katz; page 44 (bottom), Gino Santa Maria; page 45 (top), a katz; page 45 (bottom), Evan El-Amin; page 48 (top), s_bukley; page 48 (bottom), Nicescene; page 49, (top) Marcin Kadziolka; page 49 (middle), Ovidiu Hrubaru; page 49 (bottom), Sorbis; page 50, Frederic Legrand - COMEO; page 54, JStone; page 58 (middle), Joe Seer; page 59(middle), Michael Candelori; page 74, Paolo Bona.

Acknowledgements

The photo-stories 'Apprentice of Love' and 'Wrestling With His Destiny' originally appeared in My Guy magazine and can be seen in their original 1980s form in The Best of My Guy by Frank Hopkinson (ISBN 9781861059796).

Thanks to all at Portico and Pavilion Books for the continued patronage and patience.

And special thanks to Frank Hopkinson for the kind permission to re-appropriate his classic My Guy photostories

ALWAYS 100% UNOFFICIAL